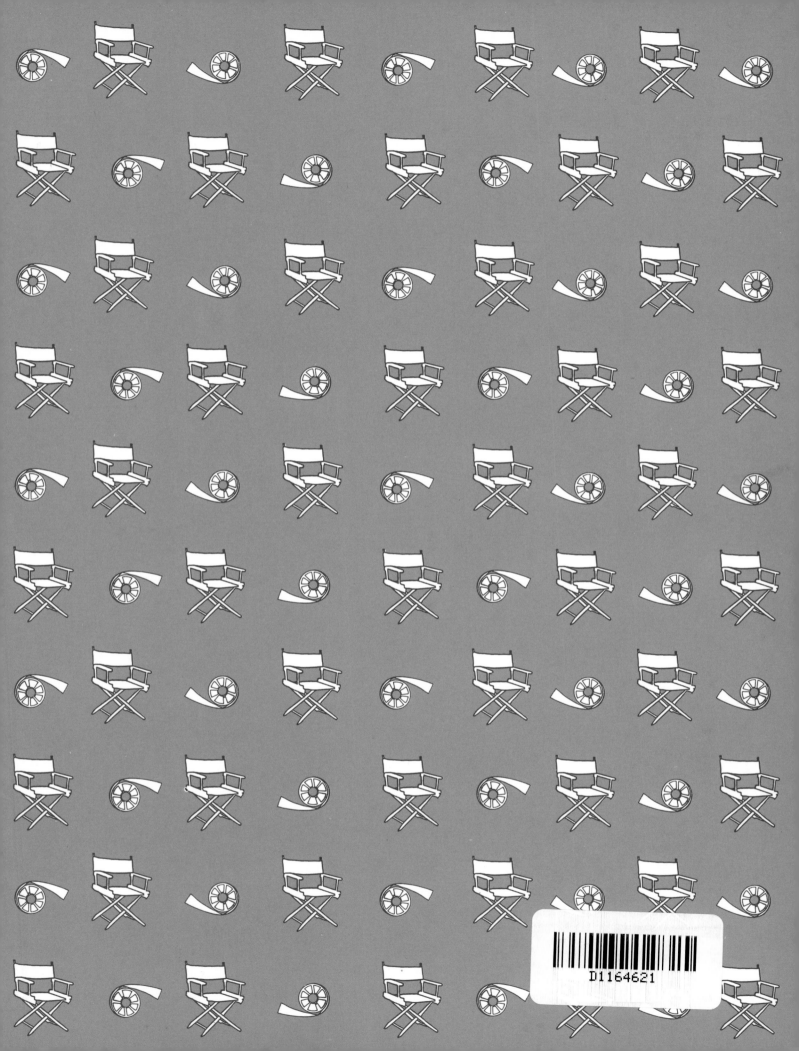

EYEWITNESS ◉ GUIDES

CINEMA

Cigarette cards

Patrick Bergin's costume for the 1991 production of *Robin Hood*

Three-strip Technicolor camera

Tape splicer for cutting film

An evil gremlin from the film *Gremlins*

Charlie Chaplin's
shoes worn in *The
Immigrant*

EYEWITNESS ◉ GUIDES

Knife with
fake blood

CINEMA

Written by
RICHARD PLATT

Vinten camera

DORLING KINDERSLEY
London • New York • Stuttgart
in association with
THE MUSEUM OF THE MOVING IMAGE • LONDON

Mechanical slide

A DORLING KINDERSLEY BOOK

Hat and jewellery worn by Faye Dunaway in *The Three Musketeers*

Project editor Gillian Denton
Art editor Christian Sévigny
Senior editor Helen Parker
Senior art editor Julia Harris
Production Louise Barratt
Picture research Kathy Lockley
Special photography Dave King
Additional photography Karl Shone, Steve Gorton

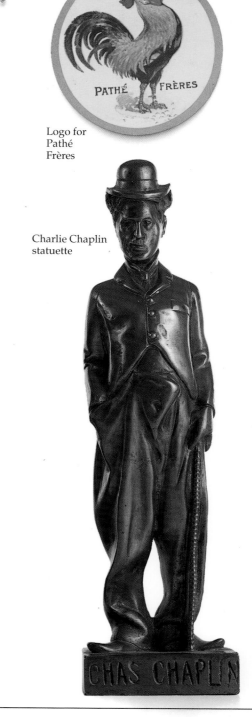

Logo for Pathé Frères

This Eyewitness ® Guide has been conceived by
Dorling Kindersley Limited
and Editions Gallimard

Charlie Chaplin statuette

First published in Great Britain in 1992 by
Dorling Kindersley Limited,
9 Henrietta Street, London WC2E 8PS

A CIP catalogue record for this book is available
from the British Library

ISBN 0 86318 791 9

Colour reproduction by Colourscan, Singapore
Printed in Singapore by Toppan

Strip of colour film

Contents

Spool of film

Light and shadow

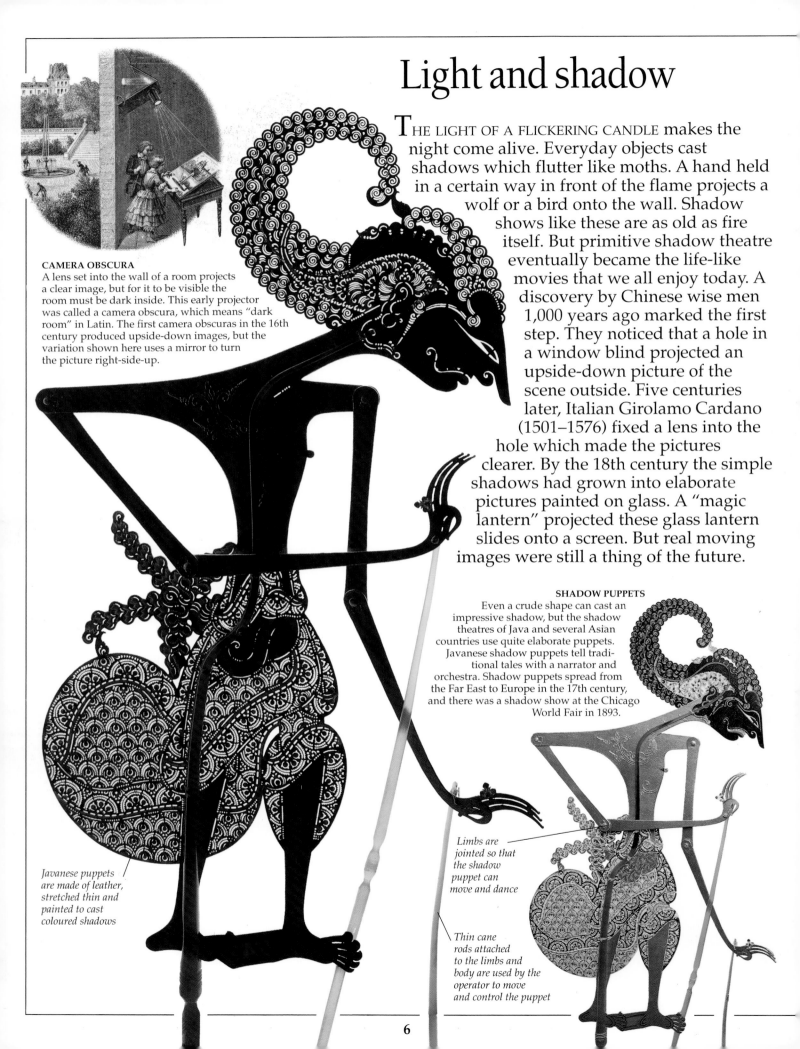

THE LIGHT OF A FLICKERING CANDLE makes the night come alive. Everyday objects cast shadows which flutter like moths. A hand held in a certain way in front of the flame projects a wolf or a bird onto the wall. Shadow shows like these are as old as fire itself. But primitive shadow theatre eventually became the life-like movies that we all enjoy today. A discovery by Chinese wise men 1,000 years ago marked the first step. They noticed that a hole in a window blind projected an upside-down picture of the scene outside. Five centuries later, Italian Girolamo Cardano (1501–1576) fixed a lens into the hole which made the pictures clearer. By the 18th century the simple shadows had grown into elaborate pictures painted on glass. A "magic lantern" projected these glass lantern slides onto a screen. But real moving images were still a thing of the future.

CAMERA OBSCURA
A lens set into the wall of a room projects a clear image, but for it to be visible the room must be dark inside. This early projector was called a camera obscura, which means "dark room" in Latin. The first camera obscuras in the 16th century produced upside-down images, but the variation shown here uses a mirror to turn the picture right-side-up.

SHADOW PUPPETS
Even a crude shape can cast an impressive shadow, but the shadow theatres of Java and several Asian countries use quite elaborate puppets. Javanese shadow puppets tell traditional tales with a narrator and orchestra. Shadow puppets spread from the Far East to Europe in the 17th century, and there was a shadow show at the Chicago World Fair in 1893.

Javanese puppets are made of leather, stretched thin and painted to cast coloured shadows

Limbs are jointed so that the shadow puppet can move and dance

Thin cane rods attached to the limbs and body are used by the operator to move and control the puppet

6

The fluted chimney lets out the heat from the candle used as a light source, but keeps stray light from spilling on the screen

Lens projects an upside-down image, so slides are inserted upside-down also, so that they appear upright on the screen

Early lantern slides were painted on strips of glass, and sliding the strip moves a new picture into view

MAGIC LANTERN

This ancestor of today's movie projectors had a simple lens, and used a candle as a light source. The magic lantern was most widely used for entertainment, but its origins were more serious: a Dutch scientist, Christiaen Huygens (1629–1693), used one to project medical pictures. Magic lanterns became more elaborate in the 19th century. Gas lights gave a brighter image, and extra lenses allowed the projectionist to fade pictures in and out.

Flick corner (pp. 8–9)

TRIUNIAL LANTERNS

Triunial, or triple, 19th-century lanterns stacked up three projectors to make possible spectacular effects. They were very expensive so only professional "lanternists" could afford them.

A flame of acetylene gas produced a brilliant white light called limelight

PHANTASMAGORIA

Belgian Etienne Robert shocked his audiences in the 1890s with his phantas-magoria show. His special lantern created frightening images of demons which appeared to advance on the audience.

Early gas-powered lanterns used dangerous mixtures of gases, so some shows ended with a bang!

The projectionist could make images suddenly appear or vanish by using the shutters on the lenses

THAT'S ENTERTAINMENT

Like today's holiday video, a lantern slide show was considered a civilised way to end a pleasant evening. A bed sheet hung on the wall made a fine screen.

Each lens projects a different picture; fading from a night scene to the same scene in daylight gives an impression of dawn

PEEP SHOW

Travelling peep shows were very popular in the 19th and early 20th century, especially amongst country people who had little or no entertainment.

Blue glass in the hinged doors allows the operator to check the flame

Whirling wheels

ROCKING THE BOAT
Moving lantern slides were common by 1750. Moving the lever on this one makes the boat roll.

WHEN WE WATCH A MOVIE, the continuous action we see on screen is a clever *illusion* of movement. For a movie is not one continuous image, but thousands of still pictures. They fly by so fast that we do not see the individual images. Our eyes merge the pictures together, and we see them as movement. The illusion works because our eyes need a little time to take in what they see. For years people wondered why their eyes were not quick enough to see fast-moving things. In 1765, a Frenchman, Chevalier d'Arcy, whirled a hot coal on the end of a rope and suggested that the glowing coal made a bright circle in the dark because its image persists (remains visible) for about one tenth of a second. But his work went unnoticed until the 1820s, when people used his discovery to make toys and other entertainments.

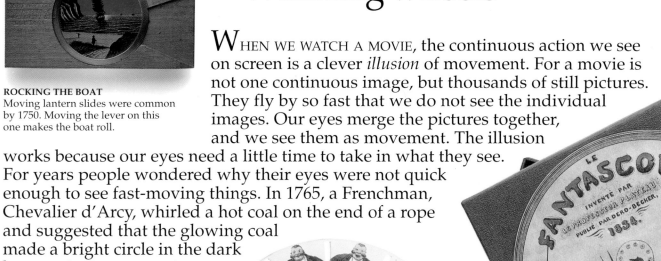

The novelty of the Phenakistoscope soon wore off, and sales of the toy dropped

The discs show a cycle of movement, so the juggler's balls stay in the air while the disc spins

In some places, such as Britain, the Phenakistoscope was sold as the Fantascope – possibly because nobody could pronounce the long name!

JOSEPH PLATEAU
Belgian physicist Joseph Plateau (1801–1883) followed up Chevalier d'Arcy's work. Through his experiments, he invented the Phenakistoscope.

PHENAKISTOSCOPE
Despite its tongue-twisting name, the Phenakistoscope was very simple. It was a slotted disc printed with a series of pictures. Each showed a moving subject, such as an acrobat, in a slightly different position. By spinning the disc in front of a mirror and looking through the slots, viewers saw the images reflected in rapid sequence and had the illusion of movement.

MICHAEL FARADAY
Although best remembered for his invention of the electric motor, English physicist Michael Faraday (1791–1867) also showed how rotating objects appear to stop when seen through slots in a spinning disc.

THAUMATROPE
The simplest toy based on the persistence of vision is the Thaumatrope, which first appeared in 1826. There are images on both sides of the disc, and spinning it on its tight string merges the images.

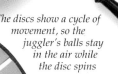

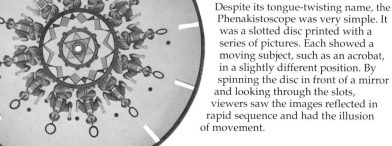

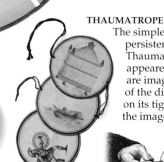

Box of spare discs

The bird printed on the other side of the disc enters the cage when the disc is spun

EMILE REYNAUD
French artist and inventor Emile Reynaud (1844–1918) created the Praxinoscope viewer, and later developed a projector for moving pictures.

FLICK FOR FUN
To see how the persistence of vision can make pictures really move, flick the page corners of this book. Turn to the last page and gather all the pages under the thumb of your left hand. Now draw your thumb slowly back, to let the pages flick down, and you'll see the picture come to life. A number of early picture-viewing novelties used this page-flipping principle including the Mutoscope (pp. 10–11).

Seen through the viewing aperture, the figures on the paper strip appear to move against the backgrounds

A simple shade reflects candle-light onto the images

Viewing cards propped up under the viewing window

PRAXINOSCOPE
Like movie projectors, all moving picture toys rely on intermittent viewing – the viewer sees each picture only briefly. Most used a narrow slit to give a brief glimpse of each picture, but this made the pictures dim and hard to see. However, in Reynaud's Praxinoscope, mirrors replaced the slits. The reflected images were then much brighter, and blended together to give a smoother impression of movement. It was a huge success.

Candle-power provides the light

The mirrors reflect the images on the paper strip

The black background of the paper strip disappears when seen through the viewing window

Viewers spin the drum by hand to make the images move

Because of the light direction, a piece of glass (not shown) reflects the background card, but since glass is transparent, the figures in the drum show through

This elaborate model of the Praxinoscope was grandly called *The Praxinoscope Theatre*

With a choice of backgrounds, the moving figures can perform as easily in a street, a park, or a circus

Each interchangeable paper strip has a sequence of 12 pictures

Snapping shutters

THUNDERING DOWN A WHITE TRACK, a racehorse snaps threads stretched tight across its path. The broken threads trigger the shutters of 12 identical cameras, so with each prancing step, the horse photographs itself. This odd scene made history in 1878, for the racehorse, Occident, was the first moving subject to be captured in a photograph sequence. The British photographer, Eadweard Muybridge, was not the first to use a camera nor to photograph movement: Frenchman Nicéphore Niépce invented photography more than 50 years earlier and pictures of slow-moving subjects were common. Even Muybridge's simulation of motion through a sequence of images was not new: toys such as the Praxinoscope had been around even longer than photography. But the way he combined these technologies was revolutionary. He built a camera shutter that opened and closed fast enough to freeze the horse's speeding hooves. As a result, Muybridge's horse, prancing in silhouette, was to lead in just ten years to the first true movies.

NOW YOU SEE ME...
Early photographic processes were not very sensitive to light, and to create a good picture required an exposure lasting many seconds. Subjects that moved during this time appeared blurred or disappeared altogether. This 1838 busy Parisian street appears empty because the camera shutter was open for more than a minute. Only one man stood still – he was having his shoes shined!

EXPOSED!
Nicéphore Niépce (1765–1833) took the world's first photograph in 1827. Taking the picture required an exposure lasting one whole summer's day, and practical photography was still 12 years in the future.

BIRDMAN OF BEAUNE
Muybridge's photographs of animals helped him study how they moved and inspired others who shared similar interests. Etienne Jules Marey (1830–1904) of Beaune, France, was studying bird flight, and asked Muybridge to photograph a bird. The experiment was not a complete success because Muybridge had designed his cameras to photograph larger subjects. Nevertheless, Marey was sufficiently encouraged to build a special camera which he could keep trained on birds in flight.

Etienne
Jules Marey

A large drum contains extra photographic plates and is removable to make the camera lighter and easier to aim

Sight for aiming just as on a real rifle

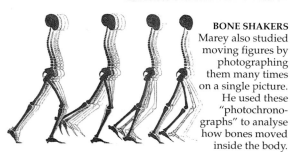

BONE SHAKERS
Marey also studied moving figures by photographing them many times on a single picture. He used these "photochrono-graphs" to analyse how bones moved inside the body.

GOOD SHOT
Marey shaped his camera like a rifle, mounting the lens in the barrel. The lens projected an image of the flying bird onto a circular or octagonal (eight-sided) photographic plate. A clockwork motor made the plate revolve, and at the same time opened and closed a shutter behind the lens. The rifle-camera enabled Marey to take 12 pictures of a flying bird in a second. The exposure for each picture lasted just $1/720$ of a second, so even the rapid wing-beats of a flying bird came out sharp and clear on the plate.

The weight of the glass plate inside the camera limits its speed to 12 pictures a second

The trigger on the rifle camera works like the shutter release on an ordinary camera

ON THE MOVE

Although Muybridge's first picture sequences were of horses, he went on to photograph a wide range of moving animals and people. 20,000 of the pictures appeared in Muybridge's 1887 book *Animal Locomotion*.

FLYING HORSES?

Eadweard Muybridge (1830–1904) worked as a scenic photographer in the far western USA before becoming interested in animal motion. He took his famous sequences to discover whether a galloping horse ever had all its feet off the ground at once. It did! Scandal interrupted Muybridge's work in 1874 when he killed his wife's lover. But a court decided that the murder was justified, and Muybridge was released.

FILOSCOPE

Movie pioneers often used complex viewers to display their pictures, but the simple flick book did the job just as well, and was in use in 1868. The Filoscope, patented in 1896, had a lever to make flipping the pages easier.

MINIMA

The small size of the pictures on Etienne Marey's discs made them difficult to see clearly, but to make larger pictures would have required a very much bigger camera, and would have introduced other technical problems.

The wooden rifle stock makes it easier to hold the camera steady

Mutoscopes were often beautifully decorated as they competed with each other for the viewing public

A placard on top of the machine announces the saucy delights inside – and the price

Viewers look through a pair of lenses at the front

Dropping a coin into the slot allows the viewer to see the sequence through from beginning to end

Turning the handle makes the pictures move

ADULTS ONLY

Mutoscope pictures offended 19th-century morals, but they were tamer than much of today's family television.

WHAT THE BUTLER SAW

Before the invention of the projector, picture sequences and very early movies could be viewed only by one or, at most, two people at a time. The most successful viewer was the Mutoscope, which an American, Herman Casler, invented in 1894. Inside was a series of cards, printed with pictures of a moving subject. Turning a handle flipped the cards, making the figure move. Early cards showed mildly sexy pictures: a woman undressing was typical. The machines bore the placard "what the butler saw" (when he peered through the key-hole of his employer's bedroom). Today, the Mutoscope is still nick-named the "*What the butler saw*" machine.

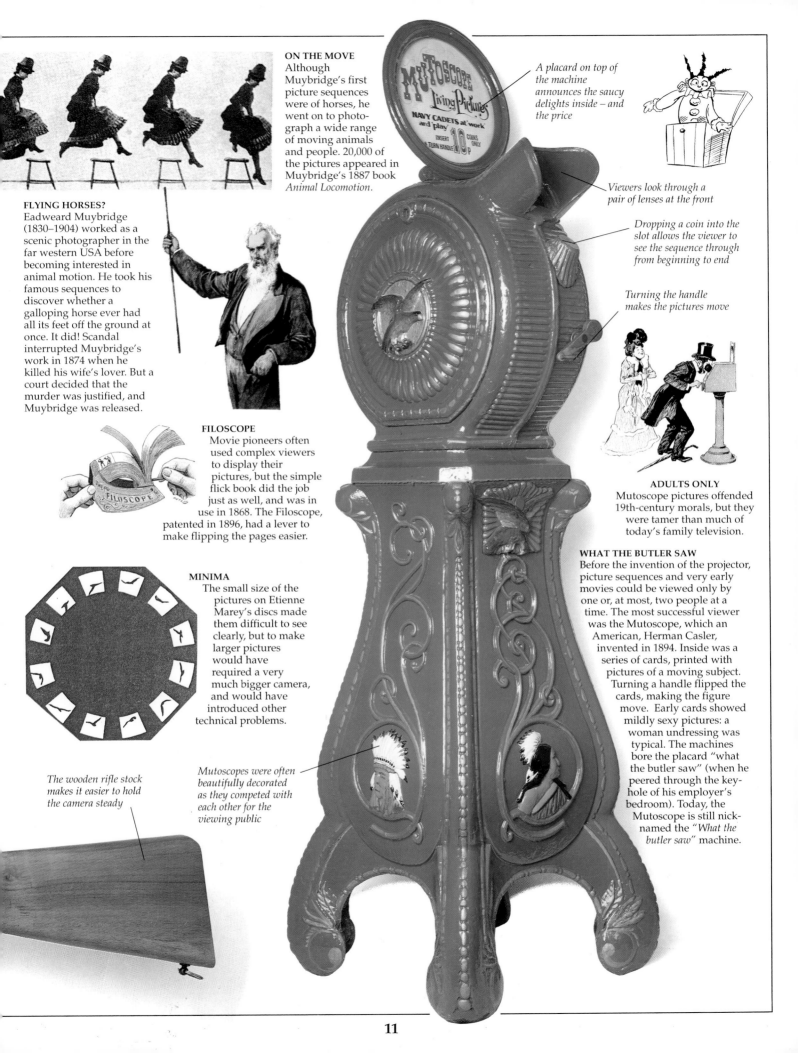

What is film?

AT EVERY CINEMA PERFORMANCE, hundreds of metres of film pass before the eyes of the audience. A minute of cinema requires more than 27 m (90 ft) of film. A full-length feature uses 2.5 km (more than 1.5 miles). Today, a whole industry exists simply to supply the enormous quantities of film that movie companies need, to process it, and to make the prints (copies) that are shown in cinemas. In the past, there have been many different gauges (widths) of film in use, but modern feature films are shot on a standard gauge of film – 35 mm. The format of the film is derived from the size of the first film, made by George Eastman of Rochester, USA. He based his film sizes on those of the glass photographic plates he was making before film became available. Starting with the biggest window glass he could find, he repeatedly halved the panes to make the sizes he required. So film we use today is based on the size of Rochester windows in 1885!

EASTMAN
George Eastman (1854–1932) brought movies closer in 1889 when he marketed flexible film. Previously, photographers had used glass plates or light-sensitive paper.

FIRST FILM
The very first "films" were not shot on film at all. Frenchman Louis Le Prince (1842–1890) loaded a roll of light-sensitive paper into the camera he made in 1888. With it, he shot pictures of traffic on a bridge in Leeds.

EDISON'S FILM
Thomas Edison originally planned to make movies on light-sensitive drums. But his assistant William Dickson instead chose to use the film George Eastman had produced for the Kodak still camera. Dickson slit the 7.6 m (25 ft) of film lengthways. Then he punched perforations in the edge to help wind it evenly through the Kinetograph camera he had built.

American inventor Thomas Edison (1847–1931)

Sprocket holes move the film through the camera so that it advances by the same amount between each frame

THE SUM OF THE PARTS
All 35 mm movie film is a standard width, with sprocket holes, or perforations, of standard size and shape. However, the size, shape, and spacing of the frames depends on the camera and lens used to shoot the film.

On 35mm film, there are 24 frames for each second of action

Modern film is made of cellulose acetate – early film was made of highly flammable cellulose nitrate

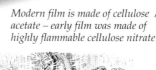

KINETOSCOPE PARLOUR
Movie-goers dropped a coin into Edison's machine to watch a film lasting just 15 seconds. The arcades housing the machines were called penny arcades, or nickelodeons, after the American nickel (5¢ piece).

Sound is recorded as a wiggly line between the picture and the perforations – devices in the projector "read" the shape of the line and convert it back to sound

English inventor William Dickson (1860–1935)

8 MM

To reduce the cost of home movie-making, cameras of the 1930s ran 16 mm film twice, making two rows of quarter-size frames. Slitting the film in two created a new format – 8 mm.

9.5 MM

The French Pathé company introduced 9.5 mm film for amateur movies in 1922. They put the perforations down the middle of the film between frames so that the frames could be wider.

35 MM

Each frame in modern 35 mm format, comes above the last, across the width of the film, which travels vertically down behind the lens of the camera or projector. However, in some early cameras, the film moved horizontally, so the pictures are positioned side-by-side, as they are today on 35 mm still film. The only camera that still uses this system is Vistavision, which is sometimes used for special effects. Most 35 mm films are shot in "Academy" format: frames are about 1.4 times wider than they are high.

Formats

The earliest movie cameras had to use wide strips of film to give a reasonable image on the screen, because film quality was poor. However, 35 mm cameras were large and heavy so when the quality of film stock improved, camera makers experimented with smaller cameras and film formats. But 35 mm is still preferred for most feature films.

16 MM

In 1923, 16 mm film was introduced for amateur movies. It was non-flammable, and the size was chosen in preference to 17.5 mm (exactly half the larger 35 mm format) to stop amateurs from slitting the flammable 35 mm film into two for use in home projectors and cameras. Today, many news films are shot on 16 mm.

70 MM

For projection in huge cinemas, 35 mm film is sometimes enlarged to make a print on 70 mm film. In the past, some films were shot using special cameras that took 65 mm film, and printed on to 70 mm; Walt Disney still use this system for films shown at Disney World.

WIDE-SCREEN

To make spectacular wide-screen movies, film makers use an anamorphic lens. This squeezes a wider-than-normal picture onto standard 35 mm film, and a matching lens on the projector stretches the picture to fill the cinema screen.

LARGER THAN LIFE

To thrill their audiences, makers of 3-D films often included shots such as logs rolling towards the camera. Sometimes the effect was so realistic that the audience would dive for cover.

3-D movies

To create lifelike (3-dimensional) depth in a projected movie, the camera must record two images through lenses several inches apart. Audiences wear special glasses so that the left eye sees the image filmed by the left camera lens, and vice-versa.

Blue lens

Orange lens

SQUID SQUAD

The ultimate wide-screen format is IMAX. Frames ten times bigger than normal are projected onto a vast curved screen, producing a spectacular, and sometimes horrific, sense of realism.

COLOURING-IN

To watch black-and-white movies in 3-D, audiences wear coloured glasses. Later systems for colour movies used grey polaroid glasses, but viewers saw double if they tilted their heads.

The lenses match filters on the projector so that each eye sees the correct image

Cameras

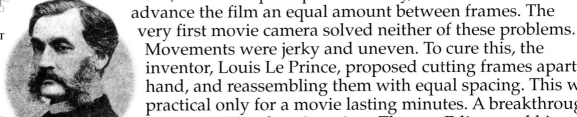

Design for Le Prince's
1888 camera

FRENCH FIRST
Three years before
Dickson's camera,
Frenchman Louis Le
Prince had shot several
short films in Britain
(pp. 12–13), using two
cameras of different
designs. Neither worked
perfectly, and Le Prince
mysteriously disappeared before
he could perfect them.

INVENTORS FACED TWO PROBLEMS in building a practical movie camera: creating smooth movement means taking at least 16 photographs a second; and to keep the picture steady, the camera has to advance the film an equal amount between frames. The very first movie camera solved neither of these problems. Movements were jerky and uneven. To cure this, the inventor, Louis Le Prince, proposed cutting frames apart by hand, and reassembling them with equal spacing. This was practical only for a movie lasting minutes. A breakthrough came in 1889, when American Thomas Edison and his British assistant William Dickson perfected a working camera. With it they made a short film of a man. According to a contemporary newspaper report: "It bowed and smiled, and took off its hat with the most perfect naturalness and grace". Dickson's simple scene charmed all that saw it, and this nameless man became the world's first movie star.

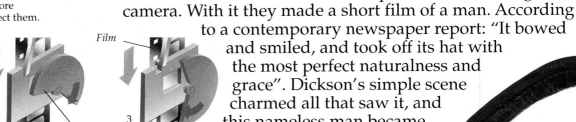

Claw

Film

1

2

Shutter

3

How cameras work

Film moves through virtually all movie cameras intermittently – with a stop-start motion. While the film is still, a rotating half-disc, which acts as a shutter, swings open to let light reach the film (1). When the shutter has closed, a claw moves forward and engages one of the film's perforations, pulling it down ready to take the next picture (2). Then the claw withdraws, and the shutter opens once again (3). This process is repeated many times – 24 a second on most modern cameras.

The handle is only for carrying the camera; during filming it is attached to a stand

A footage counter shows how much film remains

The view through the eyepiece shows what the camera will record on film

A dial on the back of the camera tells the operator how fast to crank

Cranking this handle operates the camera

Debrie Parvo camera
Side view

The Debrie Parvo is a French camera

IN A FRENZY

Until the end of the 1920s most cameras were hand-cranked: the operator (seen here on the right of the picture) turned a handle on the side of the camera to expose the film. Two turns a second was average but camera operators could turn the crank more slowly; this speeded up all the actors' movements when the film was shown. The result is the familiar jerky, frenzied action of the silent comedy.

This is an early film called *Gimme* shot at Goldwyn Studios in Culver City, California

DEBRIE PARVO CAMERA

Like many early movie cameras, the Debrie Parvo had a wooden body. This made it very light and compact compared to modern 35mm cameras (such as the model shown in use below right). The two film magazines fitted into the camera side-by-side, and the camera operator started filming simply by turning the crank on the camera's right-hand side. The Debrie Parvo was patented (registered as a unique and original design) in 1908, and remained popular with film makers for over 40 years.

MOUSE MAGAZINES

On Bell & Howell cameras, the two film spools were mounted one behind the other inside single light-tight magazines. The camera's unmistakeable outline became familiar to millions of fans from the on-set photographs that appeared in movie magazines, and even today, people associate the characteristic "Mickey Mouse ears" shape with movie cameras.

MODERN CAMERAS

As cinema has become more sophisticated, cameras have become more complex: today's film cameras are combinations of optics, mechanics, and electronics. Different cameras are built for different purposes, but some multi-purpose cameras, such as the one shown here, are compact enough for difficult location shots yet sufficiently quiet to use in the sound studio.

Sprockets drive the film through the camera

Lens mount holds lens securely

Locking knobs are marked "O" and "F" for ouvert and fermé (open and closed in French)

Crank

Simple sector shutter

The lens is very simple by today's standards

Lever which operates the lens aperture, controls the amount of light reaching the film

A rod on the side enables the operator to focus the lens from the back of the camera

Inside a Debrie Parvo camera

A number that appears in a window on the camera front shows the shutter setting

Debrie Parvo camera Front view

Flickering fantasy

THE FIRST MOVIES WERE ENORMOUSLY POPULAR, but there was never more than one person in the audience! Thomas Edison showed his films in coin-operated Kinetoscope machines, which had peep-holes for just one person to watch (pp. 12–13). Rows of the machines stood in street arcades. Edison saw his invention as a cheap toy, but others saw the potential for combining the Kinetoscope with the magic lantern.

Large audiences could watch projected pictures on a screen, so films could last longer and people would pay more to see them. In France, the Lumière brothers built a movie camera that also worked as a projector, and in December 1895, they projected films in a room underneath a Paris café. Thomas Edison was among the last to be convinced that there was a future for the movie projector. "If we make this screen machine you are asking for, it will spoil everything. Let's not kill the goose that lays the golden egg".

LUMIÈRE CINÉMATOGRAPH
Frenchmen Auguste (1862–1954) and Louis (1864–1948) Lumière were the first to invent a practical system to both shoot and show movies. To project films, they set up a powerful lamp behind the camera and cranked the film through.

Chimney lets out the heat of the lamp

Rotating shutter blanks the screen while film advances to next frame

Film could catch fire if projectionist stops turning the crank which moves the picture

Wooden knobs keep controls cool enough to touch

The Pathé projector was the first to have a stand

Screws on stand tilt the projector up

EARLY PROJECTORS
The first projectors were really magic lanterns fitted with a device to advance the film. Many used limelight (gaslight) as a light source, but as electricity became common, projectionists began to use electric arc lights instead. When a crank was turned, a "beater" mechanism advanced the film by dragging on the perforations. This caused a lot of wear, and shows were often interrupted when the film broke.

TARGET PRACTICE
Projectors were not used just for entertainment; inventors soon spotted more practical applications. Here, French soldiers improve their aim with the aid of a cinema screen, while an officer keeps score.

PATHÉ BROTHERS
Charles Pathé (1863-1957) and his brother Emile (1860–1937) built many of the projectors used to show early movies, selling them under the Pathé Frères (Pathé Brothers) name. The pair are best remembered, though, for the newsreel films their company produced from 1909 onwards. In this early advertisement, the two brothers carry projectors and reels of film, and are followed by a cock – the company's distinctive trademark.

Sewing machine

COPYCAT

In France in 1895, the Lumière brothers patented their original camera/projector based on the design of a sewing machine. The sewing machine holds the material still during stitching, then advances it quickly between stitches; similarly, a projector keeps the film still while each frame is projected on screen, then advances it quickly between frames.

Projector case

The lens enlarges films onto screens as big as 90 x 60 cm (35 x 24 in)

SHOWING NOT SEWING

The invention of non-flammable film by 1912 had made projection much safer, and film projectors became available for home use. The Pathéscope Home Cinematograph, also resembling a sewing machine, was designed to show small-scale prints of professional films, and was a huge success.

Turning this large crank shows the film

Spools hold up to 305 m (1,000 ft) of film

Removable, magnetic sound unit contains mechanism for playing magnetic sound tracks

A chimney rising from the lamp-house draws away the heat of the lamp, keeping the projection room cool

Lamphouse takes up about half the volume of the projector

Projector mechanism has interchangeable parts so it can show both 35 mm and 70 mm films

Projector has automatic shutter to cut off light if film breaks

Arc lamps need constant adjustment to ensure the brightest possible light

Optical sound head

BIGGER 'N' BETTER

As cinema developed, projectors became bigger and more advanced. Larger cinemas demanded larger pictures, and this in turn meant that the lamp in the projector had to be brighter. The Gaumont Kalee projector has a huge lamphouse to hold its bulky arc lamp. The Kalee projector was popular in main street cinemas in the 1950s; some are still in use today. Newer projectors have many more automatic functions, and in multi-screen cinemas they show films on an endless loop. A single projectionist can handle all the films for a five-screen multiplex cinema because the reels need changing only when the programme changes.

CINEMA PARADISO

The young hero of *Cinema Paradiso*, who goes on to become a famous director, is fascinated by films and befriends the local projectionist. Projection room fires were a constant risk, and in the movie a fire destroys the primitive local cinema and nearly kills the projectionist.

Hollywood in the Silent Era

BIOGRAPH GIRL
Hollywood's first named star was Florence Lawrence. Until 1910 she played leading roles in films made by Biograph studios, and was billed only as "The Biograph Girl". But a rival studio lured her away, and made her famous under her own name.

Florence Lawrence

THE INVENTION OF MOVING PICTURES was such a sensation that audiences paid just to see people walking or dancing on screen. When the novelty wore off, New York and Philadelphia film companies built roof-top studios and turned out short, cheap, dramas: films that told stories, like stage plays. But for good pictures, they needed sunshine, and they soon became tired of waiting for the clouds over the East Coast to clear. In 1910, many film makers headed west for California. There, close to Los Angeles, they found a sleepy town called Hollywood. Land was cheap, wages were low, the sun shone constantly, and there was an incredible variety of background landscapes for their movies, just a short distance away. Hollywood grew quickly – from 5,000 people in 1910 to 35,000 less than a decade later. The film people created studios, the studios created movie stars, the stars built mansions, and soon the very name "Hollywood" began to mean "Movies".

CALIFORNIA SUNSHINE
Film makers could find locations close to Hollywood to represent the desert of the Wild West, the soaring Alps of Europe, or the gentle hills of England. In the dry climate they could build indoor sets outdoors, and thus shoot entire movies without using costly lights.

An early cinema tradition was to name the chairs of the principal stars and the director

IN THE DIRECTOR'S CHAIR
Making a silent movie could be a noisy business: the camera clattered, and since there was no sound track, the director, sitting in his chair by the camera, simply gave the cast instructions as the camera rolled. On a big set, the director barked his orders through a megaphone.

Chair folds up for convenient transport on location and in the studio

NO PICNIC
Silent films required a minimum of equipment, and a tiny team to operate it. Simple location shots, such as this picnic scene with Mary Pickford shooting *Daddy Longlegs* in 1919, required only the cast, the director, the cameraman, and a couple of assistants. Cast and crew worked hard, typically arriving two hours before shooting started at nine, and filming six days a week.

OVER THE TOP
Poor-quality silent films made heavy use of caption cards, but good directors preferred instead to rely on the acting skills of the cast to tell the story. Without dialogue, actors and actresses had to perform like today's mime artists, using melodramatic gestures to suggest even moderate emotion.

Mary Magdalene in the 1926 *Ben Hur*

CAPTION CARDS
Following the plot of a film entirely without words is almost impossible, so silent films used caption cards to tell the audience what was going on. Simple captions explained the passing of time, but cards also carried long speeches, so those who could not read had to go to the cinema with someone who could, which involved a lot of whispering.

Do not think you are going to get your wicked way with me!

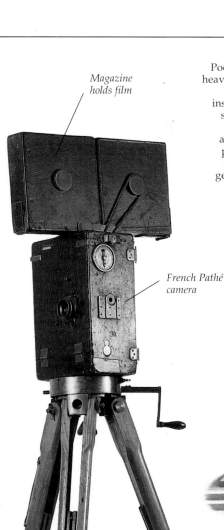

Magazine holds film

French Pathé camera

HOLLYWOOD, EUROPEAN STYLE
Though Hollywood was the centre of world movie-making for most of the silent era, many other countries had thriving film industries: Germany actually produced more feature films than the USA in 1913. In 1926, German director Fritz Lang produced his silent masterpiece *Metropolis*, a chilling vision of the future.

ON CAMERA
The hand-cranked silent camera stood on top of a sturdy tripod for most filming. The camera could tilt up and down, or turn to follow the action to the left or the right, but moving the camera during filming was difficult, and rarely attempted in the early silent years.

Solid tripod is made of wood

Tripod spreader stops legs sliding apart

POSTER POWER
Silent films came long before television, and radio advertising began only in 1922. So most people learned about new films through word of mouth, newspapers, and posters. The finest posters were as powerful as the films they advertised.

LET THERE BE LIGHT
When the sun didn't shine, movie studios used powerful electric lights. These arc lamps worked by creating a powerful spark between two carbon rods. The spark was noisy, but before the talkies arrived at the end of the 1920s, this didn't matter. The great heat of the lamps was a problem, though, and when shooting a winter scene, the cast sweated in their furs.

GETTING THE MESSAGE
Political leaders soon recognized the persuasive powers of film: in the Soviet Union, films such as Sergei Eisenstein's *Battleship Potemkin* put across political messages very strongly.

END OF AN ERA
When the talkies appeared in 1929, many predicted that the public would prefer silent films, but silent movies disappeared with remarkable speed. The last silent feature film, *The Poor Millionaire*, was released just over two years after the first talkie appeared on screen.

Stars and studios

THE EARLIEST ENTERTAINMENT FILMS were once called "cheap shows for cheap people". They were poor quality; they lasted 15 minutes or less; they had nameless actors; and admission was just a handful of coins. But by 1910, the film industry was changing. Hollywood studios (film-making companies) were creating longer, better-quality films, with named stars. The studios were run by "movie tycoons" – businessmen who had made (and often later lost) enormous fortunes producing movies. They ruled their studios like kings and hired and fired staff and stars on a whim. Stars signed exclusive contracts to appear in one studio's films. They were rewarded with enormous salaries, and millions of people followed their lives both on- and off-screen. In films, their love affairs and adventures provided romance and excitement. In real life, many stars came from humble homes, and their sudden wealth and glamorous life-styles gave fans a fantasy of escaping their own hum-drum lives.

RICH AND FAMOUS
The lives of famous film people appeared to be idyllic. Huge houses, ranging from French chateaux to Spanish haciendas, sprang up like mushrooms in the hills around Hollywood. Swimming pools, servants, cars, and parties were all an expected part of a star's lifestyle.

VALENTINO
Rudolph Valentino (1895–1926), playing an arab lover in films such as the *The Sheik* (1921), was the idol of millions of women.

GLORIA SWANSON
The career of silent screen beauty Gloria Swanson (1897–1983) began when, as a clerk of 16, she visited a film set and was asked to appear as an extra.

BEBE DANIELS
Virginia "Bebe" Daniels (1901–1971) first appeared on screen at the age of seven, and became famous as Harold Lloyd's leading lady in his silent comedies.

THEDA BARA
Famed for her sexy roles as eastern princesses, Theda Bara's stage name was a rearrangement of the letters of "arab death". At her birth in 1890 she was Theodosia Goodman. She died in 1955.

POLA NEGRI
The thick Polish accent of silent screen star Pola Negri (1894–1987), ended her career when the talkies arrived.

Renee Adoree

John Gilbert

Star treatment

In the first films, the actors playing leading roles earned low salaries and were anonymous. The "star system" began when highly paid and pampered stage actors began to appear in films. Soon cinema actors and actresses expected similar treatment – and similar salaries!

Lillian Gish

I KNOW THAT FACE
Film stars were so famous that their faces could be guaranteed to sell practically any product. Collectors' cards in cigarette packets were very popular.

BRITISH STUDIOS
British studios flourished in the 1920s and 1930s. Britain's best-known studio, Rank, was founded in the 1930s by flourmilling tycoon J. Arthur (later Lord) Rank, in order to make religious films.

CINECITTA
Italian studios were important in early cinema, but became less important as Hollywood grew. Only in the 1950s did Italian studios, led by Cinecittà, again make popular films.

GAUMONT
Frenchman Leon Gaumont, who founded the British Gaumont studios in Shepherd's Bush, west London, was also an inventor of the sound movie. In 1900, he demonstrated one of the first sound-on-disc talkies.

Mae Murray

IDOL GOSSIP
The lives of the stars became a major Hollywood industry, and the numerous film magazines were full of gossip and facts about the latest screen idol. In reality, the "true" stories were often invented by publicity agents, and real-life scandals, which would have damaged the stars, were kept out of the headlines.

UNITED ARTISTS
Movie stars did not like being "owned" by the big studios, so some stars started their own studios to have more independence. Married couple Mary Pickford and Douglas Fairbanks (above), two of the greatest silent stars, joined Charlie Chaplin and director D.W. Griffith to found United Artists, now part of MGM. United Artists financed and distributed films, but had no film studios of their own.

STAR COMPACT
Norma Talmadge (1893–1957), one of three actress sisters, decorates this powder compact.

Hollywood studios
When Hollywood began, movie making was a risky business. The businessmen who started studios didn't mind. Many came from poor families and were used to hard work. Some, such as Harry Cohn of Columbia Studios, were legendary for their coarseness. But manners didn't matter: they could spot talent, and knew what would please the public.

PARAMOUNT
Adolph Zukor, the mogul who controlled Paramount Studios, tested films by showing them to his children. He thought that if they liked them so would audiences.

MGM
"More stars than there are in the heavens" was the motto of Metro Goldwyn Mayer. Studio talent ranged from Lassie the dog to Elizabeth Taylor.

WARNER BROTHERS
Jack, one of the four Warner tycoons, once dismissed bad reviews of his films with the words "Today's newspaper is tomorrow's toilet paper".

20TH CENTURY FOX
A 1935 merger created this famous studio. Fox Studios, one of the merged companies, pioneered both sound and colour.

The arrival of the talkies

JAZZ SINGER
The first sound films were made as early as 1900, but talking feature (long) films began only in 1927 with *The Jazz Singer*. In it, star Al Jolson (1886–1950) sings several songs, and talks in two brief sequences, but the rest of the film is silent. A year later the first all-talking film *Lights of New York* was released and by 1929 the talkies had really arrived.

WARNER BROS. SUPREME TRIUMPH
AL JOLSON
IN
The **JAZZ SINGER**

Starting the projector sets film and disc running together

KALEE

Simplex 25

NO.1.

Heavy and fragile discs often broke between cinemas

Projectionist places the needle at a marked spot on the record to start the sound at the right moment

One motor drives picture and sound, so that they stay synchronized

S ILENT SCREEN STARS, like modern mime artists, became expert at expressing themselves without words. Instead, they communicated with their faces and hands, exaggerating every gesture.

Then suddenly, in 1927, the silent screen spoke. Film makers had found a practical way to record sounds as well as pictures. Movie audiences loved the new "talkies". For a while, people flocked to the cinema just to enjoy the novelty of hearing actors speaking: they even laughed at the sound of an egg frying. But the Hollywood stars were not so pleased. The extravagant gestures which had been so expressive in silence now just looked like bad acting. Worse still, some of them had strong accents which, combined with early sound systems, made them impossible to understand. For many Hollywood stars, the coming of the talkies meant the end of a glittering career. But for the survivors, it was the start of a new one.

"*Audiences are saying it, Everywhere*"

At last, "**PICTURES** *that* **TALK** *like* **LIVING PEOPLE!**"

WARNER BROS. **VITAPHONE** PICTURES

If it's **Not** *a* WARNER PICTURE *it's* **Not** VITAPHONE

VITAPHONE
To make and show successful talkies, picture and sound must be synchronized (kept in time). The Vitaphone sound-on-disc system was among the first to achieve this. Its success encouraged others, and by 1929 there were over 200 incompatible sound movie systems in use. This caused huge problems, and film makers looked for a standard system so that cinemas would need only one sort of projector. Sound-on-disc systems were soon rejected and by 1930 Vitaphone was obsolete.

SOUND PROJECTORS
All modern films have sound recorded on the film itself, but for some early films, separate discs carried the sound track, and the projector had a built-in record player. The projectionist had to match the discs with the film reels. Mistakes were hilarious, with the audience hearing women's voices when men spoke.

Large horn to amplify sound

HIDDEN HORN
Making talkies at first created great problems for film studios. There was no electronic amplification, and it was hard to keep the bulky horn of the recording equipment out of the picture, yet close enough to record sound clearly.

Edison's studio

COMIC CROONER
The French comic actor Rigadin is seen here creating the sound track for one of his films. To get round the difficulties of recording sound and picture together, most film makers first shot the film without a sound track. Then later, the actor was recorded reading, or singing, the script and music in time with the film.

The first gramophone discs were just 127 mm (5 in) across – little bigger than today's compact discs

A steel or thorn needle turns the wiggling groove of the gramophone record into sound

GRAMOPHONE
When talkies began, sound recording was already common-place. In 1878, Thomas Edison had invented the phono-graph, which played recordings on wax cylinders. However, the first sound movies used recordings made on discs – a system pioneered in 1888 by the gramophone. A mechanical linkage between the projector and the gramophone was meant to ensure that both ran at the same speed.

HE DIDN'T MAKE IT...
John Gilbert couldn't make the transition to the talkies although he was a superstar on the silent screen. His voice was high-pitched and squeaky, and audiences laughed when they first heard him speak.

SOUND ON FILM
Recording sound directly onto film ensured that picture and sound-track were synchronized. An electronic valve in the camera glowed with a brightness propor-tional to the sound level. This created the pattern of lines representing the sound track. The projector contained a light-sensitive cell to "read" the pattern and turn it back into sound.

Sound track

Whoopee (1930) was an early musical starring Eddie Cantor. 35 mm colour prints of it have survived

...BUT SHE DID
The thick accents of many European actors ended their careers when sound movies arrived, but audiences loved Greta Garbo's husky Swedish voice. She was lucky, because her voice matched her cool, mysterious image perfectly.

FLYING THE FLAG
Alfred Hitchcock (1899–1980) made the first British talkie, *Blackmail*, in 1929. Originally a silent film, Hitchcock remade it swiftly, dubbing (re-recording) the Czech leading lady who spoke little English.

Alfred Hitchcock

Anny Ondra

BOOM BOOM!
In the first talkies, actors couldn't move around much because they had to speak into microphones concealed on the set. Fixing the microphone to a boom – a long arm – solved the problem. When actors moved, the boom operator moved with them, keeping it just out of the picture above the set (pp. 30–31).

Picture palaces

IN THE GOLDEN YEARS of the movies, film stars were like kings and queens for hire: for the price of a cinema ticket, anyone could enter the world of Hollywood royalty. Movie-goers didn't need the projector to flicker into life before entering that glittering world, for the fantasy began as soon as they stepped inside the cinema door. A uniformed usher led them through a luxurious marble-lined hall the size of a cathedral, under crystal chandeliers, and up deep-carpeted stairs to their seats. Before the films started, an orchestra and ballet dancers entertained them. These cinemas of the 1920s and 1930s were so grand that people nicknamed them "picture palaces". They offered every imaginable convenience, including restaurants, crèches for children, free telephone calls, art galleries, dance floors, table tennis and billiard rooms. One cinema had a hospital; another, a chiropodist. Their aim was to encourage people to see films frequently. The tactic worked: in 1930, when the population of the USA was 122 million, Americans went to the movies 95 million times each week.

FIRST PREMIERE
When the Lumière brothers rented a room in Paris in 1895 (pp. 16–17) to show a selection of their films, only 35 people came on the first day. However, soon the cinema was a runaway success, selling 2,500 tickets a day. Cinemas quickly sprang up all over the world – less than a year later the Salon Cinématographe opened in Sydney, Australia.

ALL LIT UP
The elaborate exteriors of the cinemas of the 1920s and 1930s were every bit as grand outside as they were within. Many were built in the style of Middle-Eastern and Far-Eastern architecture, with gold-encrusted domes and minarets (mosque towers). Others had simple block-like exteriors while some were streamlined like the prow of a ship. But almost all were gaudy: by night, hundreds of light-bulbs and neon tubes lit up the buildings with flashing signs and spectacular lighting effects.

MOVIE MEALS
Cinemas catered for their audiences' bodies, as well as their minds, by installing cafés and restaurants. The type of restaurant largely depended on the clientele of the cinema, with quite grand meals on the menu of the most luxurious city centre picture palaces. Smaller provincial cinemas provided budget meals for their less wealthy film fans.

Stop keys arranged around the keyboard allowed the organist to change the sound of the notes

Seat designed so that audience could admire the organist's fancy footwork on the pedal board

THE MIGHTY ORGAN
In the silent era, a pianist provided the musical sound track that accompanied a movie, but as cinemas grew, organs replaced pianos, and by 1929, when talkies made them obsolete, cinema organs had become very grand. Bright lights decorated the organ console, the keyboard, and the organist's seat. The organ rose from the floor as the music started. Cinema organists, like Reginald Dixon, became celebrities themselves. The most ambitious organs could also provide simple sound effects.

Reginald Dixon

MOVIE CATHEDRALS
The lavishly-decorated interior of the picture palace transported the audience to far-away places. Hidden lights provided soft illumination which gradually changed colour. Special projectors created starlight and moving cloud effects on the ceiling, and some cinemas even had perfume sprayed into the air-conditioning system.

Decorative detail from the Regal

FILM FARE
Just five years before the first movies, Dr John Pemberton of Atlanta, Georgia, invented Coca Cola, so it is appropriate that millions of movie-goers quench their thirst on the drink each day. Popcorn is much older, and originated in Central America several thousand years ago.

Design for the Regal Cinema, Tooting, London

Even at the grander picture palaces, tickets were still cheap enough for working people to visit more than once a week

DECO DESIGNS
The first cinemas were simply converted music halls, but by 1910 architects were designing purpose-built cinemas. They were given considerable creative freedom, and the surviving cinema buildings from the 1920s and 1930s include some superb examples of Art Deco, the decorative style that dominated the period between the first and second World Wars (1918–1939).

ROXY
Samuel Rothafel, or "Roxy", created the greatest of all the picture palaces. His New York City Roxy cinema, which opened in 1927, seated more than 6,200 people, and had a staff of 300.

CARS AND TRAINS
The picture palace changed wherever it sprung up. Drive-in movies began in the car culture of New Jersey in the USA in 1933, and in the Soviet Union, the government built a cinema in a railway carriage to take movies to remote areas. The Agit train spread the government word by showing propaganda films.

Hollywood in Technicolor

A SILENT WORLD WITHOUT COLOUR would be a dull place, but this is all the early movies offered the public. Film makers realised from the start that their black-and-white films would look better in colour, and they went to great lengths to reproduce all the hues of nature. The very first films in colour were hand-tinted with brushes: "every photograph has to be painted, with the aid of a magnifying glass, in identical tints. The photographs are about the size of a postage stamp…" This method of colouring films was very slow, and a stencilling system soon took its place. Even stencils produced crude tints, because each scene contained fewer than six colours. From about 1900, inventors tried many different ways of capturing natural colours in the camera, but colour movies weren't really successful until 1932, when the Technicolor company produced their "Three-strip" camera. Even then, colour movies were expensive and difficult to produce, and they took over from black and white far more slowly than talkies replaced silent films. By 1954, half of all films were still made in black and white.

STENCILLED ON COLOUR
Each colour added to a black-and-white film needed a separate stencil. A team viewed the film frames one by one, and traced round the areas to be tinted, then operated stencil cutting machines. Colour quality depended totally on the skill of the operator.

VINE ST
HOLLYWOOD BLVD

HOLLYWOOD HESITATES
The coming of colour was not universally welcomed in the film capital. Many people preferred subtle shades of grey to Technicolor's over-bright hues.

Heavy magazines hold the three strips of film separately

TECHNICOLOR THREE-STRIP CAMERA
The revolutionary Technicolor camera used a beam-splitter – a special prism – to multiply the image from the lens. The beam-splitter projected separate images onto three black-and-white films, recording the subject's red, blue, and green parts individually. A special printing process put the colours back together on the film that was shown in cinemas. Although the cameras worked well, they were extremely costly to make, and the complex printing process added to the expense of making Technicolor films.

Camera has three film transport mechanisms – one for each strip of film

Technicolor cameras needed special lenses

Viewfinder window shows the camera operator what is being filmed

Light-tight door covers mechanism when camera is operating

Matt-box (lens hood) keeps stray light out of the lens

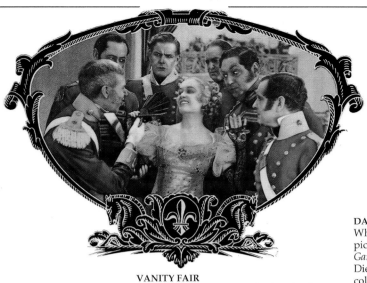

VANITY FAIR

Technicolor's first real test came in 1935, with the launch of *Becky Sharp,* a historical drama based on Thackeray's *Vanity Fair*. It was the first feature film made entirely using the Technicolor three-strip process. Not everyone liked the film or its brilliant, almost garish, colours: one critic wrote that the cast looked like "boiled salmon dipped in mayonnaise".

DANGEROUS DESERT

When colour was still a novelty, studios picked themes that made full use of it. *Garden of Allah* starring Marlene Dietrich was one of only four full-colour Hollywood features made in 1936, and its sets and costumes were sumptuous and brilliant. It was sold with the slogan "Dangerous love in a desert paradise!"

FAMOUS FLAMES

Not all colours looked equally good in Technicolor. Reds and yellows were especially brilliant, so fire looked fantastic, and for a while it seemed as though every Technicolor film had to have a fire scene. In the 1939 classic movie, *Gone with the Wind*, the whole of Atlanta burns.

CARY GRANT

Dashing star Cary Grant was famous for his sophisticated air and great comic talent. He made his Technicolor debut in 1946 as Cole Porter in *Night and Day*.

INGRID BERGMAN

Her success playing a lead role opposite Humphrey Bogart in the black-and-white classic *Casablanca* won Ingrid Bergman her first colour role in the 1943 movie *For Whom the Bell Tolls*.

BETTE DAVIS

Movie legend Bette Davis made her first Technicolor film, *The Private Lives of Elizabeth and Essex* in 1939 at the height of her popularity.

MARLENE DIETRICH

The box-office popularity of Marlene Dietrich ensured that she appeared in colour almost at the start of the Technicolor era: she starred in *Garden of Allah* (above).

Three-strip Technicolor camera

TECHNICOLOR TRAIL

The first film to be shot entirely on location using the heavy Technicolor equipment was the 1937 Paramount film *The Trail of the Lonesome Pine*. But the film won no prizes for its colour. *Newsweek* magazine wrote that "Unnatural as it is, the colour does no serious damage to the picture."

PUTTING ON WEIGHT

Technicolor cameras were extremely heavy and cumbersome, and were useless without a sturdy tripod or dolly. Because of this limitation, early Technicolor films were shot almost entirely in the studio.

Making a movie

SAMUEL GOLDWYN
Polish glove salesman Samuel Goldfish (1882–1974) changed his name to Goldwyn, and became one of the USA's greatest producers.

Producers

Producers are in control of the production. When they agree a date for filming, pre-production starts. This phase involves hiring actors, buying props, and booking studio time. So when the camera starts rolling, every detail of the film has been planned, down to the final seconds of the schedule.

DINO DE LAURENTIIS
This Italian producer (born 1919) was expert in giving the public what they wanted and in co-operating with foreign companies to make his movies.

Oɴᴇ ꜰɪʟᴍ ᴍᴀᴋᴇʀ describes the magic of the movies as "turning money into light". Making films is very costly because it involves so many people and so much work. The most obvious work takes place during production – when the film is being shot. But almost as much work is needed before and after this crucial phase. Producers oversee the whole process. They decide which films to make, find the money to finance them, and make most important planning decisions. The producer hires a director to take most of the creative decisions about the film. Together, they plan the movie, and develop the idea into a screenplay (a movie script) with a budget and shooting schedule.

Many films begin as books

Each number represents a different scene

TAKE ME TO YOUR LEADER
The director is responsible for the look, sound, and feel of the film, but may do other jobs as well. American director Spike Lee has acted in his own films, and has also been the producer of some of them.

During the shooting of a film, the director or the writer often adjust the script for greater realism or impact

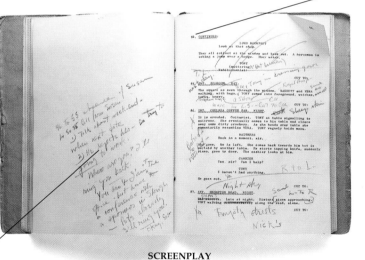

Screenplay for *The Servant* by Harold Pinter

SCREENPLAY
The screenwriter turns an idea or a book into a screenplay that actors can perform. Often this will be revised many times.

HOLLYWOOD GOLDMINE
The cost of even a low-budget movie is enormous, and today's typical Hollywood feature film costs around $15 million, excluding publicity costs. Much of the money goes on salaries. The stars are paid enormous fees, but shooting a film also requires the work of many highly skilled specialists. Even a simple studio sequence with just two actors might require as many as 50 other technicians and support staff (pp. 30–31). Some of them, such as the camera crew, work directly on the film. But others, such as catering staff, are just as important to the production.

Storyboards help the director visualize the scenes

This 1921 cheque to Gloria Swanson was enormous at a time when American industrial workers earned about 50 cents an hour

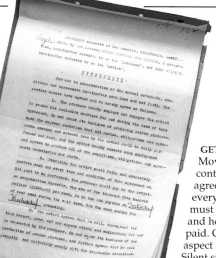

CASTING

Deciding which actors will play which parts is called casting. The cast is so important to the success of a film that the screenplay may even be written specially to suit one particular star. Casting popular star Whoopi Goldberg in the lead of *The Color Purple* helped ensure that the movie was a box-office hit

Whoopi Goldberg

GET IT IN WRITING

Movie lawyers draw up contracts (written agreements) to make sure that everyone knows what they must do, when they must do it, and how much they will be paid. Contracts can cover every aspect of a star's behaviour. Silent star John Gilbert's contracts stated that he should never do anything which would offend public morality.

STORYBOARD

An important stage in the planning of a movie is the creation of a storyboard. This is like a picture-book, in which a small picture several centimetres across represents each shot. Underneath, there is a description of the action, often with some of the dialogue. Storyboards can be worked out in considerable detail, like this one from *The Wizard of Oz*, but some movie companies produce much more sketchy storyboards, often without colour so that the storyboard can easily be photocopied for distribution to everyone involved. A single movie requires many storyboards, sometimes nearly 1,000.

Scenes are heavily annotated

Watercolour has been used to illustrate this storyboard. Often, other media, such as gouache, ink, or paint, are used

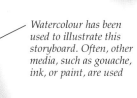

PRETEND PARIS

Constructing a spectacular set can be enormously expensive, but it can work out cheaper to build part of Paris in the studio, than to ship the cast and crew to France. Set building is essential when part of the film is set in a place where location photography would be impossible or uncomfortable.

SELLING IT

Promoting and advertising a film can cost more than making it. Posters, such as this one advertising an Indian film, play a large part in giving the film an identity in the eyes of the public (pp. 62–63).

BACKROOM BOYS

After principal photography is complete, there's still plenty to do before the audience sees the film. This work, which includes editing the film, is called post-production (pp. 48–49).

Splicer for cutting film

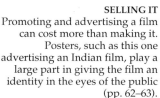

The studio at work

THE DIRECTOR BARKS OUT "ACTION!" and the filming starts. Powerful lamps flood the set. The hubbub of conversation in the studio turns into the silence of anticipation. Cast and crew concentrate on getting the perfect take (shot). All eyes are on the actors, as they play the scene – perhaps for the twentieth time that day. When the director calls "Cut!", the cameras stop, and everyone relaxes for a moment, waiting to see if the take is perfect. If it isn't they must repeat it until the director is satisfied. Technicians swarm over the set: the gaffer and best boy adjust the lights; the chief grip moves the camera; the prop master checks the set; make-up artists repair smeared faces; wardrobe staff adjust costumes; and sitting at a console of dials, the mixer monitors sound levels. The work of the studio is bewildering to watch, because there are so many people. Yet everyone has their own special task. When the cameras roll again, cast and crew put aside their individual thoughts and work together as one, like the gears of a well-oiled machine.

STUDIO CITY
Some large film companies own their own studio facilities, but more and more, a film company will rent studio space only for the duration of a production. Studio complexes offer film makers every facility they need during production, including labs, props stores, projection rooms, editing suites, and even stables and a zoo for animal stars. The largest, Universal Studios at Orlando, Florida, has its own police and fire departments.

Focus puller and camera operator both have seats at top of crane

Crane raises camera above the actors' heads

Heavy weights counterbalance the camera and crew

Chains stop crane from bouncing up when crew and camera are removed

Powerful light can be adjusted to give broad or narrow beam

"Barn doors" help shape the beam from the light

Tyres allow crane to move smoothly across studio floor

Tall stand can lift lights high above the set

Crab dolly can move in any direction, even sideways

Although some jobs, such as director and producer have been explained, there are others which are also vital but less well-known.

Best boy Assistant to gaffer
Boom operator Positions and operates microphone
Chief/key/head grip Moves camera
Continuity person (Script supervisor) Ensures make-up, costumes etc. don't change between shots
Director of photography (Cinematographer/First cameraman/ Lighting cameraman) Responsible for lighting, composition, choice of camera, lens and film – in fact, the "look" of the film

First assistant cameraman (Focus puller) Maintains camera, changes lenses and magazines, operates focus control
First assistant director Controls day-to-day functioning of the set
Gaffer Chief electrician
Grip Moves equipment on set
Location manager Finds suitable locations and clears their use with owner
Mixer (Sound recordist) Person on set in overall charge of sound recording
Production manager (Line producer) Person who controls the day-to-day budget

Second Assistant cameraman (Clapper loader) Loads magazines, operates clapperboard, and performs other camera tasks
Set decorator Finds props and decorates the set
Set designer Designs the set using sketches and models
Still person Takes still photographs of the production
Wardrobe Responsible for care and repair of costumes throughout the production

ON SET

Sometimes it is easier to create outdoor scenes in the studio than to shoot on location. To make possible the construction of vast sets which simulate the world outside, a studio can contain an enormous stage (the area where the set is constructed). At Pinewood Studios in Britain, the world's largest stage is 102 m (336 ft) long. Sets built there have included a seascape complete with a 600,000 tonne oil tanker and three full-size submarines. Not all studio sets are built specifically for each production: low budget films in particular may re-use sets built for another movie. Traditional Hollywood Westerns, for example, inevitably included a frontier town, probably with a scene in a saloon, and at least one in the sheriff's office. In Hollywood's heyday a big film company might churn out 30–50 movies a year – many of them Westerns – so building Main Street from scratch for each one would have been very wasteful.

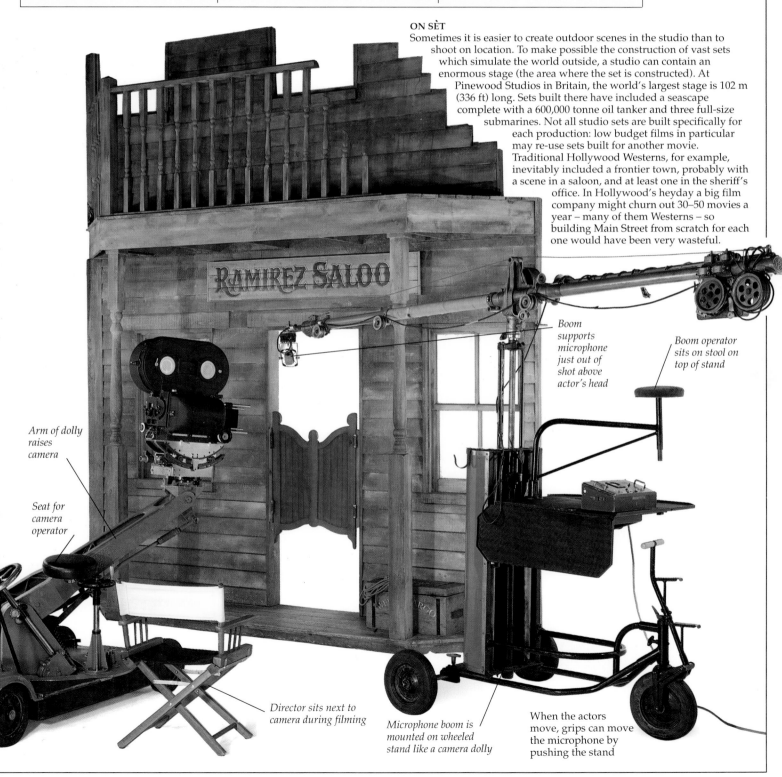

Arm of dolly raises camera

Seat for camera operator

Director sits next to camera during filming

Boom supports microphone just out of shot above actor's head

Boom operator sits on stool on top of stand

Microphone boom is mounted on wheeled stand like a camera dolly

When the actors move, grips can move the microphone by pushing the stand

On location

Maps and photographs help the art director find suitable locations

WHEN BUILDING A SET would be expensive or impossible, film makers close the doors of the studio. Instead of filming in the controlled environment of a sound stage, they take their cameras outside and use the real world. Filming out of doors using a city, a jungle, a river, or a mountain as a backdrop is called location photography. Some films are shot entirely on location; others may have just short location sequences to set the scene for footage shot in the studio. For example, if a character walks into a hotel lobby from the street, a film crew may shoot on location to show the action outside the hotel, then film interior sequences in the studio. Location filming does not always mean visiting the real place where the action is set. For instance, many cities have a "Chinatown" area where shops and even street signs look like similar streets in Beijing. Crews may shoot location sequences there, rather than visiting China.

BIRD'S EYE VIEWS
On location, there are no ceiling or walls to limit the movements of the camera. On a crane, the camera can start with a close-up of a single face, then soar up for a broad view, as in this scene from *Goodbye Mr. Chips*.

FISHY BUSINESS
Underwater sequences are often shot in a glass-sided, studio tank, but for realism there's no substitute for the ocean. *Twenty Thousand Leagues under the Sea* required special equipment to keep the camera dry during the submerged filming.

A STUDIO WITHOUT WALLS
One aim of location photography is to increase a film's sense of realism. However, reality does not always look as good as viewers (or the director) expect it to. To make the location fit the screenplay more closely, film makers add props, and often supplement sunlight with electric lamps. In this location sequence from *A Passage to India*, powerful arc lamps top the stands (right of picture) and provide the "sunlight". A further lamp alongside the camera is covered by a sheet of diffusing material to soften its beam. This lamp puts light into the shadows so that they do not appear inky black on screen. Another lamp just visible (left of picture) does the same job. The black screen – called a gobo – just in front of it, is used to shade parts of the scene so that light does *not* fall on them.

CLOTHES MAKETH MAN?
Location shooting is tough on costumes, which need on-the-spot repairs if they are damaged. Repairs to elaborate costumes, such as Rex Harrison's Caesar outfit for *Cleopatra,* would be difficult, so the wardrobe department packs several identical costumes. In this picture, the actor relaxes on the set with his wife.

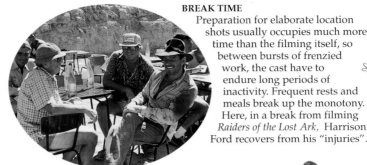

BREAK TIME
Preparation for elaborate location shots usually occupies much more time than the filming itself, so between bursts of frenzied work, the cast have to endure long periods of inactivity. Frequent rests and meals break up the monotony. Here, in a break from filming *Raiders of the Lost Ark,* Harrison Ford recovers from his "injuries".

HOLLYWOOD LOCATIONS
Today "on location" means almost any outdoor scene, but in Hollywood's early years, virtually every scene was shot outdoors. The Hollywood area was still countryside when Charles Ray and his staff were filming in the 1920s, so if they wanted a farmyard location like the one shown above, they wouldn't need to travel far to find it.

CONTINUITY
Location shots filmed at different times and places must match exactly if they appear on screen one after the other. Making sure that they match is called continuity. For example, the audience would notice if an actor appeared sun-bronzed in one shot, and pale-skinned in the next. So if the two shots are filmed weeks apart, make-up may have to hide the actor's tan in one of them, or fake it in the other. Continuity staff make elaborate notes and take photographs to ensure that every detail of costume and make-up is unchanged. In this still from *The Fourth Protocol,* the continuity girl (sitting down left) advises the make-up artist who is adding the final touches to the actor's face.

YOU'LL NEVER WALK ALONE
A walk in an empty landscape such as this seashore in *Valley of the Dolls,* is not easy to simulate in the studio. But despite the appearance of solitude, the cast is far from lonely, for they have the crew for company! Here, at least four people pull the trolley supporting the camera and lights *and* their operators, while the boom operator walks alongside. Tyre tracks and footprints in the sand do not matter because they will be out of shot.

GEE UP!
When an actor drives a car or, as in this shot from the Australian film *My Brilliant Career,* a buggy, the camera travels alongside in a separate vehicle. If the horses are not in the shot, the camera car itself tows the buggy; hoof noises are added later.

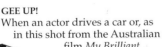

Making faces

In the make-up artist's magic box there are pleasant dreams of youth and beauty. There are bad dreams of growing old and ugly. And there are terrifying nightmares of turning into a werewolf or demon. The make-up artist delivers these and other transformations with the aid of latex (a kind of rubber), wigs, powders, and pots or tubes of colour. Make-up lets the mature actress play a young woman, and it allows an actor to become 50 years older in scenes just a few minutes apart on screen. The script may call for a famous person from the past, such as a queen or a president. Then it's the make-up artist's job to transform the actor into a convincing likeness of the character. Applying screen make-up requires a lot of skill, because the audience must believe that the faces and hair of the cast are entirely natural. This is easy when the camera films a scene in long shot (from a long way off). But when an actor's face fills the screen, every detail must be perfect for a successful illusion.

Body make-up is specially resistant to smearing, so that it does not mark costumes

Creme foundation

BASE FACE
The plaster cast of the actor's face is used as a base for adding jowls and bags in ageing. Moulds are taken from the cast to create small pieces of foam which can then be fitted to the real face.

Make-up base (foundation) covers the actor's face creating the overall skin colour

Creme and cake rouge

Translucent powder hides skin shine and sets make-up

HOW TIME FLIES!
A grey wig, highlights, and shadows make a young woman look middle-aged. Darkening eye sockets, cheeks, and temples sinks these areas as age does, and a fine brush adds wrinkles.

CORN GORE
A make-up artist can create on-screen injuries using only latex and lining colours. Coloured corn syrup simulates blood. But elaborate special effects such as those being made here for *An American Werewolf in London* require moulded foam rubber to simulate the inside of the body.

Liquid eyeliner outlines the eye

Lipstick

A wide range of brushes and disposable sponge tips are used for applying colour and painting the face

Liners are used to add colours, shadows, and highlights

False nails

Thick Dermacolor make-up lightens an actor's stubble, and helps to hide scars

When actors wear a rubber skullcap to simulate baldness, this make-up blends the cap colour with the scalp

False eyelashes

LEIA'S LOCKS
The hairstyle created for Carrie Fisher as Princess Leia in *Star Wars*, allowed the character to look well-groomed in all circumstances.

A Streetcar Named Desire

Désirée

Viva Zapata

The Teahouse of the August Moon

ROLE MODELS
In his screen roles, Marlon Brando has completely altered his appearance many times. These examples span just five years of his early career. For some roles he needed very little make-up, but for his role in *Teahouse*, Brando wore a wig and foam pieces around his eyes.

FACE OF FEAR
In Stanley Kubrick's 1971 film *A Clockwork Orange*, the leading man, Alex, wears dramatic make-up. His painted face terrifies the victims of his attacks.

Rouge

Creme foundation

Sponge for applying make-up

Eyelash brush

Latex nose

A stipple sponge is used to age an actor. When dipped in make-up, the open texture of the sponge helps to create broken veins

Ready-made moustaches

Hair pins

Grey wig

Moustaches, beards, and wigs are often made from the hair of Chinese people

Spirit gum, made by dissolving natural resin in alcohol, holds facial hair in place

False beard

Plastic tape applied to the eyelids can make Western actors look oriental, although a latex fold is usually needed for close-ups

Liquid latex has many uses. Life-like scars, wrinkles, and skin swellings can be created

HAIR DRESSING
Hair takes time to grow, so wigs, hair pieces, false beards, and moustaches, are used instead. They also ensure that an actor looks identical from one day to the next.

Dressing up

THE HIGH-TECH SPACE SUIT of a film astronaut looks very different from the elegant gown of an 18th-century screen heroine, but both costumes do the same job. They help the audience forget that they are watching an actor and help them believe that they are seeing reality – from the past, present, or future. Film actors did not always wear special clothes for the camera: in early silent films they wore their own clothes, or rented from theatre prop houses. By the 1920s, though, film studios had their own costume departments, partly because street clothes were not suited to movie technology. Early film could not record colours accurately, so the colours of clothes had to be specially chosen. When talkies began, the microphones amplified the rustling of some materials, so costume designers began to use soft knitted fabrics. Today, in big-screen close-ups, accurate detail is essential, so modern costumes are meticulously researched, and carefully sewn so that they are totally convincing on screen.

Contemporary portrait of Queen Elizabeth I in London's National Portrait Gallery on which the designer based the royal costume

FEET FIRST
International costume hire companies keep as many as 15,000 pairs of shoes in stock, and enough boots for an army of 10,000. Their stock ranges from authentic Roman sandals to foot-wear of the present day.

FIT FOR A QUEEN
In Hollywood's heyday, accuracy was less important than atmosphere. But today's costumes have to be correct to the last bow. Glenda Jackson's costume in the film *Mary Queen of Scots* was a true copy of Elizabethan royal attire.

DAY AT THE RACES
English designer and photographer Sir Cecil Beaton (1904–1980) created sumptuous and authentic costumes for the 1964 production of *My Fair Lady,* for which he won an Academy Award (Oscar). Audrey Hepburn wore this ravishing white lace outfit for a scene where the heroine, Eliza Dolittle, visits the races.

HEAD DRESSES
Hats, like all other aspects of costume design today, have to be as accurate as possible. The eras since World War II have been the first in history where head gear has not been everyday wear.

Beaton revived needlework and embroidery styles that had been current when G.B. Shaw wrote *Pygmalion,* on which the film is based.

Monroe in the famous ukelele scene in *Some Like it Hot*

SOME LIKE IT HOT
Blonde screen idol Marilyn Monroe played sexy Sugar Kane in the 1959 film *Some Like it Hot.* Australian designer Orry Kelly (1897–1964), made her costumes as revealing as he dared.

Sketch for Branagh's *Henry V*

MADE TO MEASURE
Stars in new films have their costumes specially created, as Kenneth Branagh did for his role as Henry in *Henry V,* but lesser parts are often dressed from the stock of costume hire companies. As many as 750,000 civilian costumes and uniforms hang from their racks. Actors find outfits that roughly fit, and staff then alter the clothes for an exact fit.

A STITCH IN TIME
Today's film techniques show clothes in such detail that tailors and dressmakers often hand-stitch historical costumes; the stitches of a sewing machine would look too neat.

GONE WITH THE WIND
In the famous 1939 film *Gone With The Wind,* star Vivien Leigh wore many versions of the same dress. In scenes of Atlanta burning, she changed 27 times, starting with a dress in perfect condition, and ending with it filthy and ripped.

Vivien Leigh as Scarlett O'Hara wearing widow's weeds

Sets and props

WITHIN THE FOUR WALLS of a studio, film makers create storm-tossed oceans or snow-covered mountain peaks; they simulate the surface of the moon; or they transport actors back in time to ancient biblical cities. These illusions are possible through the magic of the set – the studio scenery – and the props, or properties – the accessories that provide authentic detail. Studio sets can be simple or elaborate, but they are never bigger than is needed to convey the desired atmosphere. If the script calls for a close-up of an actor sitting in the sweltering heat of an Indian summer, the film crew might build just the corner of a room, as here. Details that will be out of focus (blurred) on screen are merely suggested by painted backdrops or shadowy cut-outs. Parts of the set that the audience cannot see are omitted altogether. Elaborate scenes featuring many actors may require vast sets, and when the set grows too big to fit in the studio, building continues out of doors.

TORCHBEARER
Huge sets were built for the early epics. The ancient Egyptians were a strong influence on set designers.

BUILDING BIG
The Incredible Shrinking Man was filmed using specially made sets and props in ever increasing sizes. On screen, the film creates the illusion that the props are a constant size while the actors shrink! Small props play a role in ordinary films: placed at the back of a set they appear to be farther away than they really are, making the set look deeper.

ELEPHANTINE

The vast set of the 1916 movie *Intolerance* made it the most expensive film of its time. Director D.W. Griffith created Babylon on Sunset Boulevard in the Hollywood sunshine, and filled the city with a cast of 60,000. The 27 m (90 ft) high set stood for two years after the movie was finished, but was eventually demolished because its wooden structure was a fire hazard.

DRAWING A CROWD

Before carpenters and painters can set to work, the production designers make elaborate plans and drawings to work out exactly what the set should look like. Designer John de Cuir created this richly detailed view of late 19th-century New York for the 1969 movie *Hello Dolly*, winning the film an Oscar (Academy Award) for art direction and set decoration.

SPANISH ROME

The biggest film set ever built reproduced a section of ancient Rome on a site just outside Madrid, Spain, for the 1964 epic film *The Fall of the Roman Empire*. The vast set measured 400 x 230 m (1312 x 754 ft) and involved the construction of 27 life-size buildings, some of them soaring up almost 80 m (290 ft). 1,100 people laboured for seven months, erecting 350 statues and more than 600 concrete columns. Despite the ambitious set, the movie was a flop, and lost millions for its producer Samuel Bronston.

For shots where even this vast set was not big enough, model-makers created a small-scale replica of the ancient city

FOR REAL

Sets have to look completely authentic. On a feature film, the art director works with a set dresser to ensure that everything the audience sees is appropriate, and comes from the right era. Together, they instruct the prop master, who actually locates all the necessary items. Props may be specially made for a production, but often the prop master will hire or buy authentic items, including genuine antiques for a historical drama.

PAINT AND PLYWOOD

The only important part of a set is the side the camera sees, and what appears to be solidly built masonry is often a flimsy construction of flat canvas, painted to look like brick or stone. Beyond the rickety walls of this convincing street scene can be seen the modern buildings of the film studio.

Living dangerously

LEAPS FROM HORSEBACK, dramatic sword fights, escape from fires, car crashes; these exciting sequences in the cinema are called stunts. They look really dangerous on screen and many *are* dangerous to perform, but a stunt must be as safe as possible. Careful camera angles make the action look more hazardous, and special effects can fake death and injury. But stunts are still too risky for leading stars to do, so another, specially trained actor called a stuntman (or woman) stands in for the star. They wear the same make-up and clothes and usually the camera films the stunt from a distance so the face cannot be clearly seen. To complete the illusion, the camera films close-ups of the star. Mixing these shots makes it appear to be the star who performs the stunt.

IN THE FIRING LINE
Fire sequences are very dangerous. They are filmed in short takes lasting just a few seconds. Then the crew douse the stuntman's burning clothes with fire extinguishers.

FALL GUY
Many stunts consist of falls from as high as 27 m (90 ft). Air mattresses help break the fall but stuntmen also wear body armour.

Shoulder pads

Elbow and forearm pad showing imitation blood

Knee and shin pads prevent damage to the legs

Some body armour is specially made, but stuntmen also use protective clothing from sports such as ice hockey

Hip pads are essential for falls on stairs

Spinal injuries can end the stuntman's career; this pad protects the lower spine

For execution by hanging, a special harness, or jerk jacket, saves the stuntman's neck and jerks his body with grisly realism

Kevlar oversuit provides extra protection when whole body is exposed to fire

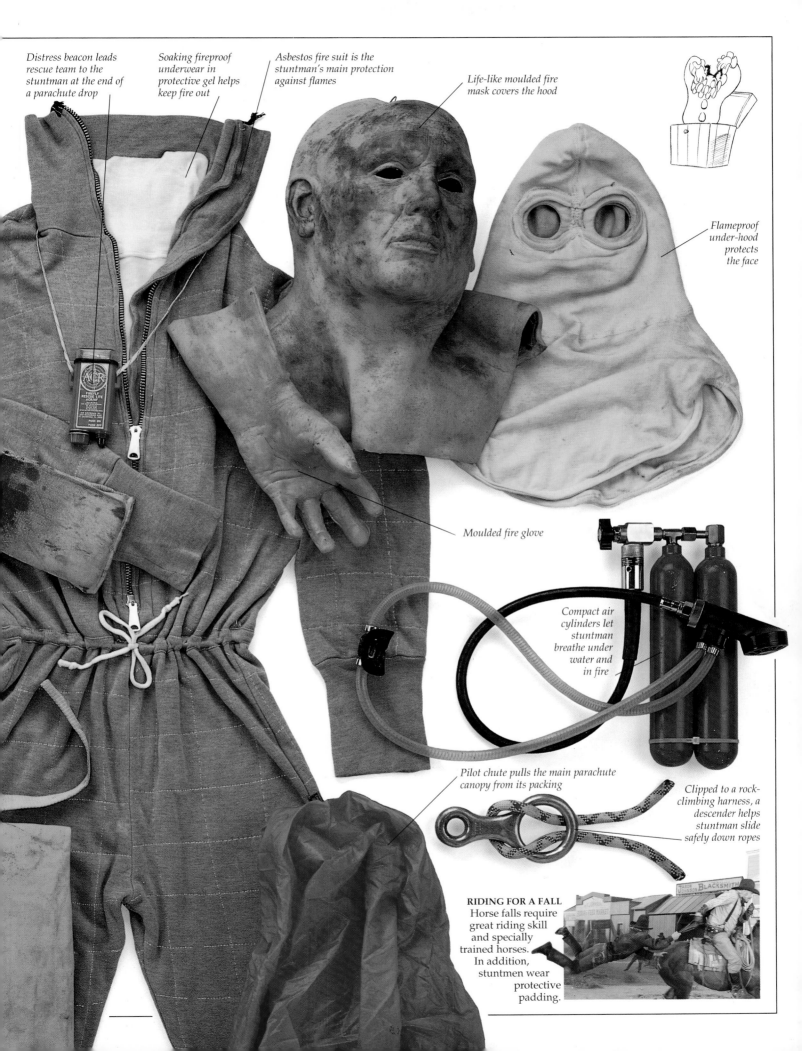

Distress beacon leads rescue team to the stuntman at the end of a parachute drop

Soaking fireproof underwear in protective gel helps keep fire out

Asbestos fire suit is the stuntman's main protection against flames

Life-like moulded fire mask covers the hood

Flameproof under-hood protects the face

Moulded fire glove

Compact air cylinders let stuntman breathe under water and in fire

Pilot chute pulls the main parachute canopy from its packing

Clipped to a rock-climbing harness, a descender helps stuntman slide safely down ropes

RIDING FOR A FALL
Horse falls require great riding skill and specially trained horses. In addition, stuntmen wear protective padding.

Special effects

CRASH! A FLOOR COLLAPSES leaving the hero hanging hundreds of metres up. Boom! Buildings explode in balls of fire. Rat-a-tat! Bullets rip through a speeding car. Special effects make possible all these exciting sequences. They are the tricks and techniques that film makers use when the skills of make-up, costume, and the stuntman are still not enough to make a scene convincing. Even the newest films rely on some surprisingly old special effects. Hurricanes are easy to fake with hoses or fans. Flames and bombs come from pyrotechnics like big fireworks. And unbelievable backgrounds are the work of a matt artist, who paints them on glass. But at their most advanced, special effects use computer graphics to fake the impossible. Technicians "build" scenes on screen. They start by drawing crude "wireframe" models; then they render them – apply a "skin" of life-like textures and shadings. Finally, they use the computer to animate the screen models. The result is so convincing that the audience won't know they are watching a computer simulation, not a live actor.

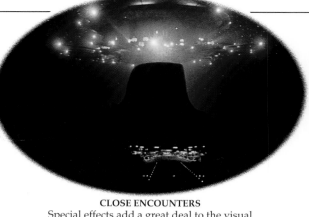

CLOSE ENCOUNTERS
Special effects add a great deal to the visual drama of a movie and for some film makers they have become a sort of trade mark. The stunning effects in Steven Spielberg's film *Close Encounters of the Third Kind* made it a huge box office success despite a weakish plot.

Speed of fan is variable

GETTING THE WIND UP
To create a breeze on set, technicians use a wind machine, which resembles an oversize desk fan. A wind machine this big can simulate anything from a light breeze to a gale on a small set in the studio: larger sets might use several wind machines.

Cage stops objects (or actors) from being injured by fan blades

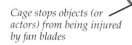

Weather forecast

Weather is an important part of the plot in many films and is the star of a few, such as *The Hurricane*. Special effects provide wind and rain with hoses and fans, and salt on the ground or on actors' costumes resembles snow; for falling snow film makers use plastic chips, chopped feathers, gypsum (dry plaster), and even bleached, untoasted cornflakes.

Creating strong winds on location requires a much larger fan; the biggest wind machines are powered by aircraft engines

IT NEVER RAINS BUT POURS
Gene Kelly (born 1912) would have looked somewhat silly singing the title song of *Singin' in the Rain* on a dry day, so the special effects department provided the necessary weather. For location shooting the local fire department often provide pumps and hoses needed to spray the cast with realistic rain; on a set, a rain standard (a tripod-mounted sprinkler) creates rain over a small area. Larger sets use clusters of sprinklers.

Heavy stand prevents wind machine from blowing itself over

A HAIL OF BULLETS
To create realistic bullet wounds when actor James Caan died in ferocious gunfire in *The Godfather*, his clothes were studded with squibs (small smokeless explosive charges) which a technician fired electrically. The compressed-air gun (below) created lifelike bullet marks on the car body and the building behind.

Shoulder stock

Gauges indicate when air pressure is right

Sight helps technician take aim

Gun has trigger just like real firearm

Hose supplies air from a compressor or cylinder

HIGH FLIER
To create the illusion of flight, an actor poses in front of a brilliant blue screen while a wind machine flaps his hair and cloak. Later an optical printer (pp. 44–45) replaces the background with a sequence shot from the back of a low-flying aircraft.

COMPRESSED TO DEATH
All guns – even "toy" air rifles – are dangerous and can cause injury, so special effects' technicians have developed unusual techniques to simulate gunfire harmlessly. They created a machine gun powered by compressed air which fires soft gelatin pellets. Filled with blood, and fired onto an actor's bare skin, the pellets burst, giving the grisly impression of a bullet wound.

No smoke without fire
Special effects make possible not only smoke without fire, but also fire without smoke. For a controllable blaze, sets incorporate flaming forks – gas jets which burn with real flames that can be extinguished when the director shouts "cut". Explosive charges do many jobs: the biggest create huge balls of fire, but squibs (tiny charges fired by electric power), create realistic bullet wounds when detonated.

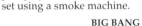

SMOKE SUPPLY
To create smoke, mist, or fog in the studio, technicians use mineral oil, which they heat and then pump by hand across the set using a smoke machine.

BIG BANG
Special effects technicians often have to get a scene right first time, because a single take destroys their work, as in this shot from *Body Heat*.

Cap indicates colour of smoke in cylinder

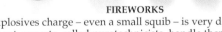

FIREWORKS
Any explosives charge – even a small squib – is very dangerous, and on the film set, experts, called pyrotechnicists, handle them to ensure safety. They detonate the flares, flashes, and bangs by passing a small electric current through the wires at the top of the charge.

Behind it all
To cut the cost of set building or location photography, special effects' technicians create painted or projected backgrounds which replace the set or add to it. For example, in a long shot of a vast castle the set might be only a few metres high; the remainder of the castle is painted onto a sheet of glass positioned in front of the camera during filming.

HANGING AROUND
By filming the background and main action separately, and combining them later, it is possible to shoot daring sequences without risk to the actor, as in this scene from *Blade Runner*.

REAR PROJECTION
With passing traffic and roadside scenes projected onto a blank backdrop, driving sequences can be realistically staged in any convenient studio. Here the special set looks out of proportion, but the movie camera will correct the distortion.

Models and animatronics

SCALE MODELS, PUPPETS, AND MOTORISED ROBOTS are the film maker's mechanical toys, but they have a serious purpose. They take the place of an actor, a vehicle, or a creature when creating or filming the real thing would be difficult, costly, dangerous, or downright impossible. Movie models look stunningly realistic on screen, and as life-like as any member of the cast, but not always as convincing when you see them on the set. Model makers only bother with the side that faces the camera, so often the controls and insides are clearly visible from the back, and models that are in the distance may be crudely finished and lacking in detail. Movie models take many forms. Using tiny models a film maker can shrink a giant set to fit on a table top. Creature puppet models are completely obedient (unlike the animals they simulate). They can even take the form of imaginary aliens from undiscovered planets. Some life-sized models are a cross between a puppet and a costume: the actor inside gives the model character, while the puppet skin supplies the fantasy.

KING KONG
In the 1933 movie *King Kong*, a monster ape terrorises New York. Kong was actually a 60-cm (23-in) high model with a jointed metal frame. An ape's skull and a covering of foam rubber and rabbit fur added realism.

Actor John Hurt and the Dog in *The Storyteller*

SHAGGY DOG STORY
Lying by the fireside, the Dog asks the Storyteller questions that the audience might want answered.

More than 20 motors control the features of the face

The Dog in British TVS and Channel 4's *The Storyteller*

IT'S A DOG'S LIFE!
Performing dogs learn some clever tricks, but none can talk like this model! The Dog is a puppet operated by a puppeteer (puppet operator) out of sight below the floor. The puppeteer also uses a joystick to control motors that operate the Dog's eyes, nose, and mouth.

ADORABLE ALIEN
In Steven Spielberg's fantasy movie *ET*, several small models stood in for the extra-terrestrial at different points in the film.

Radio control allows puppeteer out of shot to operate the whole figure without cumbersome cables

Motor was contained in the shell in the early version of the turtles

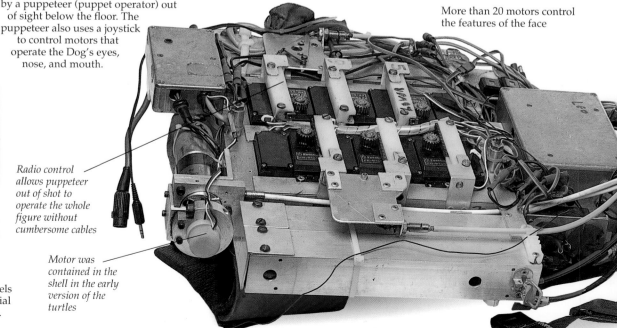

MINI MODELS
In a battle scene for *The Empire Strikes Back*, towering snow walkers carry troops into action. Building them at life size was impossible, so model makers created replicas at several miniature sizes. These tiny models appeared in the distance; larger replicas were created for close-ups. They moved by stop motion: the camera filmed one frame at a time, and the animators moved the models between frames.

BIG TIME
Small-scale models are obviously impractical if the script requires an actor to climb inside, so some models have to be full size, like this spacecraft in the gantry of Cloud City from *The Empire Strikes Back*.

MOTION CONTROL
Filming stunningly realistic space chases, such as those seen in *Star Wars*, requires a special technique called motion control. The individual spacecraft models move very little; instead the camera moves towards them on rails, filming each model individually under computer control, against a blue background. So that the craft can move closer or further apart, the camera films each separately, and the background of stars requires yet another piece of filming. Finally, an optical printer assembles all the shots into a single sequence.

OPTICAL PRINTER
Many special effects rely on the seamless joining of sequences shot at different times and places. The optical printer makes this possible. It contains two to four projectors, and an eleborate movie camera which re-photographs the films loaded into each projector, combining their images on a single frame.

Animatronics
Creature models can be moved by stop-frame animation like the snow walkers at the top of the page, but increasingly they are filmed normally and operated by an actor and a puppeteer. The actor wears a creature costume, but does not control the creature's expression. This is manipulated by a puppeteer who moves the mouth and other features by cable or radio control. Jim Henson's Creature Shop who pioneered the technology, call it "animatronics".

Eyes open and close and move left and right and up and down

Eyebrows move independently

Mouth is controlled by many motors so that turtle can talk in a very life-like way

SHELL SIZE
In the workshops of Jim Henson's Creature Shop, the actors who play the turtles, carefully try their costumes for size. Technicians take casts of the actors' bodies so that the costumes fit perfectly.

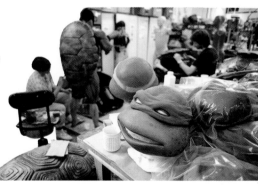

Mask made of foam rubber so it weighs very little and is highly flexible

Raphael

Computer technology allows one puppeteer to control every function – earlier models needed as many as six operators

TURTLE MASK
Each creature has two heads: one is capable of a wide range of expressions, controlled by the puppeteer; the other, a stunt head, has fixed expressions, and is used for long shots, and other scenes where movement is not needed.

Sound and score

THE SOUND TRACK OF A MOVIE is vitally important. However, dialogue (the actors' speech) only occupies a third of the sound track. The score (the accompanying music) and sound effects are at least as important to the film. A surprising amount of the sound is added after photography is complete. Sometimes the reason is obvious: no director wants an orchestra on the set as well as the cast and crew. But why replace authentic sound recorded on the set with new dialogue and effects recorded in the studio? The reasons are simple: the microphone records unwanted sound, such as traffic noise, along with the actors' voices; and often, sound effects just don't sound natural when the movie is shown. So, weeks after filming is complete, actors go back into a sound studio to loop their dialogue (re-record their lines); and technicians add specially recorded sound effects or brief snatches of sound from a library.

When silent movies were shown in small cinemas, a hard-working pianist provided the only sound

FIRST ON TRACK
Fritz Lang's film *Siegfried* was the first to have a synchronized sound track. The film had a musical score but no dialogue when it was shown at the Century Theatre in New York in 1925.

DREAM THEME
Brilliant music makes for successful films, and sometimes the music lives on long after the film is forgotten. The theme tune that Bing Crosby (1904–1977) sang for *White Christmas* is still played today, and helped the film become the year's biggest box office hit when it was released in 1954.

FROM THE BEGINNING...
Today, orchestral musicians can perform individually or in small groups to record tracks of film music. The many instruments can then be mixed down (joined together) in any combination to make a single music track. But in the past, the whole orchestra had to watch the screen and play together as if performing at a concert.

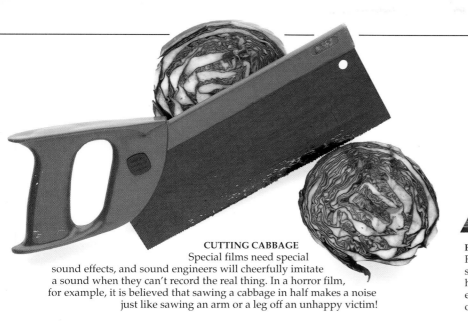

CUTTING CABBAGE
Special films need special
sound effects, and sound engineers will cheerfully imitate
a sound when they can't record the real thing. In a horror film,
for example, it is believed that sawing a cabbage in half makes a noise
just like sawing an arm or a leg off an unhappy victim!

FLOOR SHOW
For adding authentic footsteps to a
sound track, post-production studios
have special areas, equipped with
every kind of indoor and
outdoor surface.

DUBBING AND LOOPING
When a film appears in a country where
the audience does not speak the language
in which the film was originally made,
the dialogue may be dubbed (replaced
with a translation in the local language).
Usually the actor who dubs the dialogue
is not the actor who performed in the
film. The dubbing actor watches a loop of
film, and reads the lines, as far as
possible, in time with the lip movements
of the actor on screen. Using a similar
technique, called looping or post-
synchronization, actors re-record their
own dialogue
when the
sound track
recorded on
set is of low
quality.

SOUNDING OFF
The final sound track
for a film may be a
mixture of more than
40 sounds, each
recorded separately.
For the final mix-down
creating the stereo
sound track that is
heard in the cinema, a vast
multi-tape recorder plays all
the individual tracks together, and
records the finished version.

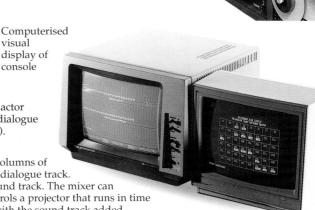

ONCE MORE UNTO THE BREACH...
When *Henry V* appeared in France, French actor
Gérard Depardieu (born 1948) dubbed the dialogue
of leading actor Kenneth Branagh (born 1960).

Computerised
visual
display of
console

MIXING CONSOLE
The sound mixer sits at a huge console to create the final sound track for the film. The columns of
knobs and sliders each control an input – an existing source of sound such as the film's dialogue track.
By altering the controls the sound mixer fixes the loudness of each input on the film sound track. The mixer can
change other qualities of the sound, by adding echo, for example. The console also controls a projector that runs in time
with all the sound inputs, so that the sound mixer can see what the film will look like with the sound track added.

Putting it all together

A FILM IS NOT FINISHED when the crew pack away their equipment and the cast heads for home. A huge amount of work is still to be done before the film reaches the screen. After each day's shooting (filming), messengers rush exposed film to a laboratory, which produces a rough copy or print of the sequences. The director watches these "rushes" every day and picks out the best. The sound track, recorded on special tape, is carefully labelled and stored. When the filming is finished the editor goes to work. The editor's job is to cut up the individual, disjointed sequences, then link them in the right order so that the shots tell the story in the best way. Working closely with the director and other artists and technicians, he or she also adds the sound, the special effects, and the titles, which make the film the polished and professional film viewed in the cinema.

Negative

Positive

PROCESSING

Film shot in movie cameras is negative film, similar to the film you might use in a still camera to take snapshots. At processing laboratories (labs), the film passes through processing machines, which develop the negative. Other machines make a positive print for the director to view and the editor to cut. When the cutting is complete, the lab makes a release print for distribution to cinemas.

Positive cutting print

Pulling down the handle trims excess tape and punches new perforations

Wax pencil used to mark up film

CUTTING AND SPLICING

To join pieces of film together, the editor uses a tape splicer. This has a small cutting blade, with pins which help to position the film, so that the cut goes exactly across the space between frames.

Lines, drawn two perforations either side of the clap, mark the correct frame

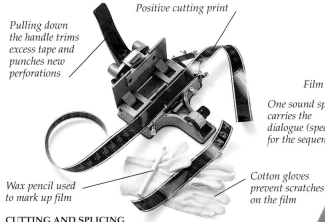

A cross marks the corresponding frame on the sound track

MIX 'N' MATCH

Sound track and screen image must be exactly synchronized (kept in time) or actors' lip movements will not match their words. So using a synchronizer, the editor's assistant marks sound-track and film with a wax pencil. The marks indicate the exact frame where the clapperboard closes.

Small screen shows a clear image of the film

Lamp in picture head projects image onto screen

Film spool

One sound spool carries the dialogue (speech) for the sequence

Cotton gloves prevent scratches on the film

Controls for sound volume and tone

Turning this knob shows the film at normal speed, or winds it forwards or backwards at high speed

EDITING TABLE

The editor views the cuts at an editing table (above). Horizontal platters at either side of the table hold the film and the sound track that accompanies it. The editor aligns the synchronization marks with the sound and picture heads visible in the centre, to ensure that the sound track will start at exactly the same moment as the picture. Then, operating the large knob at the front of the table, he winds the film back and forth through the machine, projecting the shots on the screen and playing the sound track through the speaker.

IN STYLE
The editor works very closely with the director to decide the order of shots and how long each should stay on screen. The films of Japanese director Akiro Kurosawa (born 1910) are edited with many long-lasting shots, giving his films a measured pace and rhythm. The film *Ran* (above) is typical of this style of editing.

CLAPPERBOARD
To synchronize sound and picture, the cameraman films a clapperboard at the start of each shot. Slamming shut the striped bar makes a brief "clap" that can be heard as a growl when the sound track is played slowly. The start of the growl must line up with the first frame, which shows the clapperboard closed.

SOVIET SUPREMO
Russian film director Sergei Eisenstein (1898–1948) was also a masterful editor. He pioneered the exciting technique of cross-cutting. This involves showing short fragments from two different sequences, so that they seem to be taking place at the same time.

Loudspeaker to play sound track

BINNING IT
Films consist of so many sequences that it is easy to lose track of where each one is. So the editor and assistant have to organize everything methodically. Circular cans hold most of the film; labels on the cans and on leaders (pieces of blank film spliced to each sequence) identify the shots and their corresponding sound. The shots required for immediate use hang from hooks on a rack. Their loose ends trail in a cotton bag, which keeps the film clean and unscratched. Next to each shot hangs its sound track, on magnetic tapes perforated just like the film.

Controls for film motors

Other sound spools carry music or sound effects

Film is stored loose in cans

Tape label on rim identifies the contents of each can

Film is wound onto spools or cores when needed; split spools mean that film can be removed without being unwound

Coming to life

CHARACTER FORMING
Cartoon characters start life as the roughest of pencil sketches on paper, with no colour and only primitive movements. In successive stages, animators add more and more detail, to create a character that looks and moves like a real squirrel.

At an early stage the animator adds squirrel features to the basic head shape

I MAGINE DRAWING a picture, then watching it come to life before your eyes! Sketched figures dance, trees blow in the wind, and planes zoom across the sky. This is not fantasy, for animated films, or cartoons, really are drawings, brought to life by the magic of cinema. In addition to movie magic, animation demands planning and hard work. For each second of action, a team of artists creates at least 12 pictures; there are some 65,000 pictures in a feature film. To reduce the work, animators plan out every sequence in minute detail, so that they draw static subjects only once. For example, backgrounds usually stay still, so the animator makes just one background drawing, and then concentrates on the actions of the figures moving in front. In traditional animation, moving figures are drawn on clear cellulose acetate film (cel), so that the background is visible through the unpainted areas. But more and more, animators use computers to bring their characters to life on screen.

WALT DISNEY
In 1937, American producer Walt Disney (1901–1966) made *Snow White and the Seven Dwarfs*, the world's first full-length animated film in colour and sound, and transformed the world of animation. Earlier cartoons were usually short films shown before a main feature. After Disney (shown above with some of his famous creations) many animated films were shown as main features.

Circular disc rotates so that artwork can be turned making drawing easier

Desk is lit from behind so that animator can see several overlaid images, even on paper

Animator can see how far squirrel has moved between first and last cels

Peg bar keeps cels aligned

Each cel carries one drawing of the squirrel or any individual part of it that moves

Yogi Bear

HANNA BARBERA
Bill Hanna (born 1910) and Joe Barbera (born 1911) met in 1938 and created the famous *Tom and Jerry* cat and mouse cartoons. They went on to invent many more cartoon characters, including Yogi Bear. Hanna and Barbera characters are animated very simply and clumsily compared to those of Disney, but their low budget films won a huge new audience for animation.

SLOTTING INTO PLACE
To produce an effective, smoothly moving picture, the animator makes sure that each drawing in the film differs from the one before by exactly the right amount. This is done using a registration system – an arrangement of pegs that slot through matching holes punched in every picture. By laying each cel of the sequence over the preceding cel, the animator can see how much the figure has moved.

EXTREMES AND IN-BETWEENS

Animators start by drawing the most important actions – the extremes – and draw the in-between stages later. Here, the animator would have drawn the squirrel's take-off and landing before the rest of the leap. At an earlier stage he decided how long the leap should last on screen. Each second of action requires twelve drawings, and this decides how much the figure must move between frames.

Later in the sequence the flower moves, so it is drawn on the cel

THE FIRST CARTOON

Emile Reynaud (pp. 8–9) created the first animated films even before there was a satisfactory method of making normal (live action) films. Reynaud painted his animations, called *Pantomimes Lumineuses*, on long strips of clear plastic, and projected them using a special machine.

Background drawing on paper lies underneath all the layers of cel

Exposure sheet tells the camera operator the correct order for photographing cels

Colours are mixed, as an incredibly wide range of colours is required

HIBBERT/RALPH

COLOURING-IN

On a large-scale animated film, the animator only has time to create pencil sketches of the action. An army of helpers traces the outline drawings onto the front of the individual cels and paints colour onto the back. This colouring is not always easy, because the plastic is a greenish-grey colour. When cels are stacked on top of each other, the density of the pile make the same paint appear a different colour on the top and bottom layers. So the paint-and-trace artists use a slightly different palette of colours for each layer.

When paints are mixed, an enormous quantity is mixed at a time so that a colour lasts throughout the production

Cels must be very carefully numbered and indexed to keep them in the right order

SYLVESTER

The personality of a successful cartoon character must be very strong. To achieve this, the character must look, sound, and behave the same way in every film. Sylvester, the star of many Warner Bros. cartoons, always had the voice of Mel Blanc (1908–1989).

Trace artist uses Indian ink in a special pen that gives a line of constant width

Cels are made of soft plastic, and are easily scratched

Everyone working with the cels wears cotton gloves to avoid marks

Cut-off fingers facilitate drawing

Continued on next page

ADDING COLOUR
Once the line drawing on the front of the cel is complete, the colours are filled in on the reverse side.

NO SHADE
Usually a single colour fills each area surrounded by a black line, because it is hard to make shading identical from one cel to another.

SQUIRREL SOUNDS
Squirrel's adventure would be dull in silence, but by the time the animation has reached this advanced stage, a sound track has already been prepared.

Other techniques

Traditional cel animation looks great on screen, but is complex, expensive, and requires a large team of workers. So animators constantly seek alternative ways of bringing their characters to life. Many of the most creative of these techniques have emerged from studios of animators who want to be more involved with the picture and sound the audience sees and hears. Direct animation, in which the artist creates pictures directly in front of the camera, with clay, pins, or other media, means the "artwork" changes between frames, each frame altering or erasing the one before.

Jírí Trnka

COMPUTER ANIMATION
Computers can cope with many essential tasks, like in-betweening or colouring frames, which are tedious for animators to carry out, and they can make animated films look more like real life than drawings ever could. But they also introduce some enormous technical problems. Sophisticated computer animation needs very expensive equipment, and expertise in computer programming. The most successful computer generated films have been quite short, like the Oscar-winning *Tin Toy*, which John Lasseter and William Reeves produced in 1988. The film tells the story of baby Billy (above), and a musical toy.

Norman McLaren

MODEL MAKER
By filming small models frame-by-frame, and moving them between each frame, animators can make the models appear to move. Czech animator Jírí Trnka (1910–1969) became expert at this technique, often using wooden models. Models can be animated either by preparing a separate skeleton for each position of the model, or by bending a model with flexible joints.

LOOK, NO CAMERA
Not all animators need a camera to record their work. British-born, Canadian film maker Norman McLaren (1914–1987) pioneered the technique of marking directly onto the film. In many of his films with the National Film Board of Canada, McLaren drew on clear strips of 35 mm film leader, or scratched clear lines into black film, perhaps colouring some of the lines. He even created sound by drawing an optical sound track onto the film.

PIN HEADS
Direct animator Pierre Drouin uses thousands of pins in a special board to create his pictures. Pushing in the pin makes a white area; pulling it out makes it black.

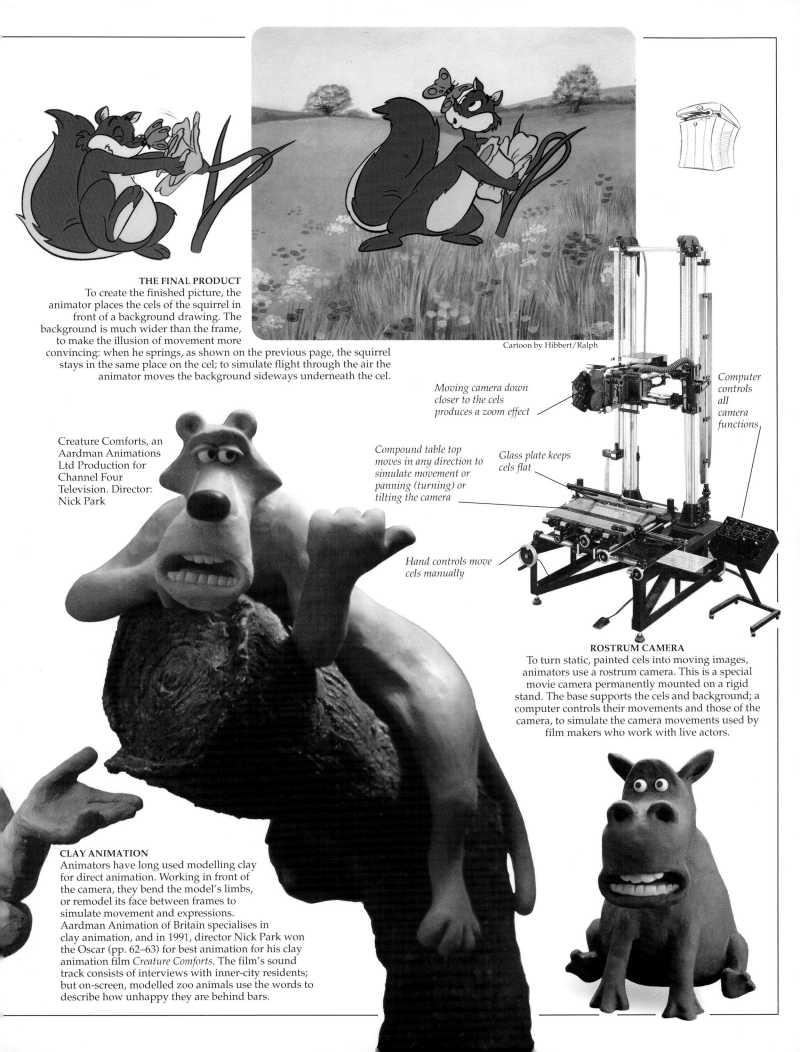

THE FINAL PRODUCT
To create the finished picture, the
animator places the cels of the squirrel in
front of a background drawing. The
background is much wider than the frame,
to make the illusion of movement more
convincing: when he springs, as shown on the previous page, the squirrel
stays in the same place on the cel; to simulate flight through the air the
animator moves the background sideways underneath the cel.

Cartoon by Hibbert/Ralph

*Moving camera down
closer to the cels
produces a zoom effect*

*Computer
controls
all
camera
functions*

Creature Comforts, an
Aardman Animations
Ltd Production for
Channel Four
Television. Director:
Nick Park

*Compound table top
moves in any direction to
simulate movement or
panning (turning) or
tilting the camera*

*Glass plate keeps
cels flat*

*Hand controls move
cels manually*

ROSTRUM CAMERA
To turn static, painted cels into moving images,
animators use a rostrum camera. This is a special
movie camera permanently mounted on a rigid
stand. The base supports the cels and background; a
computer controls their movements and those of the
camera, to simulate the camera movements used by
film makers who work with live actors.

CLAY ANIMATION
Animators have long used modelling clay
for direct animation. Working in front of
the camera, they bend the model's limbs,
or remodel its face between frames to
simulate movement and expressions.
Aardman Animation of Britain specialises in
clay animation, and in 1991, director Nick Park won
the Oscar (pp. 62–63) for best animation for his clay
animation film *Creature Comforts*. The film's sound
track consists of interviews with inner-city residents;
but on-screen, modelled zoo animals use the words to
describe how unhappy they are behind bars.

Make 'em laugh

Making someone laugh is easy; amusing a hundred people requires skill and timing as well as a sense of humour; but it takes a comic genius to make millions of people laugh in cinemas around the world. Humour on screen is especially difficult because comedians cannot change the gags or their timing to suit the audience, as they can in a theatre or club. The first screen comedians got their laughs from slapstick: fast-moving, rough-and-tumble comedy that relied on sight gags – visual jokes. The arrival of sound allowed comedians to entertain cinema audiences with the rich fund of jokes that they had rehearsed for years on stage. Today, screen humour takes many forms. Much of it, like the first silent comedies, is just for harmless amusement. But some, such as social comedy, has a serious side: though the antics on screen make us laugh, they also remind us of our own faults, and point out things that are wrong with society.

CLOWN KING
Charlie Chaplin (1889–1977) is the best-loved comedian of the silent screen. He appeared in almost 70 short films and 11 feature-length comedies.

NATIONAL INSTITUTION
Some comic films work best in just one country. The many *"Carry on…"* films have always been incredibly successful in Britain, but they have never done well in other countries. This could be due to the difficulties of translating humour or just to the very British nature of the films.

LAUREL AND HARDY
Thin Stan Laurel (1890–1965) and fat Oliver Hardy (1892–1957) were one of the few comic duos who achieved fame in the silent era, and continued with the talkies. Offstage, Stan wrote the gags; onstage his ideas got them into hilarious trouble.

The tramp's trousers are much too big because Chaplin borrowed them from fellow comedian Roscoe "Fatty" Arbuckle

DOUBLE TROUBLE
Bud Abbott (1895–1974) and Lou Costello (1906–1959) met in 1931, and worked together for a quarter of a century as a brilliant comic team. Short, plump Costello was the funny man who told jokes; tall, thin Abbott the "straight" man who was the butt (victim) of them. This formula for humour is still in use today. Abbott and Costello did not invent it, but they were the first comic pair to use the technique successfully on screen.

Chaplin's shoes were nailed to the ship's deck in The Immigrant *to enable him to lean as the ship lurched*

The tramp's shoes are size 14 and borrowed from another comedian, Ford Sterling, who is also much bigger than Chaplin

The bowler hat belonged to Arbuckle's father-in-law

PYTHONESQUE
The hugely successful *A Fish called Wanda* was influenced by a British television comedy series of the 1960s and '70s called *Monty Python's Flying Circus*. Both had a very original, anarchic (chaotic), and zany humour.

THE LITTLE TRAMP
Charlie Chaplin is best remembered for the character of a tramp that he created in 1914 for his second film *Kid Auto Races in Venice*. The tramp suffers all kinds of poverty and hardship, but never loses his sense of humour. Chaplin's little, loveable tramp laughed at a world that was often cruel, and helped cinema audiences to laugh at their own misfortunes. The comic star created his costume from whatever he could find in the nearest dressing room. He borrowed the coat and trousers from two fellow comedians who were playing cards, and made his moustache by trimming down a piece of crêpe hair.

STAND-UP COMICS
In films such as *Coming to America* Eddie Murphy makes us laugh by the funny situations he gets into. The one-line gags (very short jokes) for which he is most famous are a reminder of his early career as a stand-up comic – someone who stands up in a club or cabaret to make audiences laugh by telling humorous stories.

BLACK COMEDY
Black comedy, such as the Spanish director Pedro Almodóvar's *Women on the Verge of a Nervous Breakdown* finds humour in serious subjects.

Silent comedian Chester Conklin lent Chaplin a coat for his tramp costume

Only the cane was Chaplin's own

SLAP IN THE FACE
Stage comedians of the 19th century amused their audiences by slapping each other with a wooden paddle, called a "slapstick". Many of the gags in the early silent comic films relied on similar forms of simple humour, and such movies are known as slapstick comedies. The custard pie gag, where an actor gets a pie in the face during the course of a scene, amuses everyone. Today, paper plates and synthetic cream are usually used. In the film *Bugsy Malone*, children played adults and custard pies were much in evidence.

Custard pie

Getting away from it all

FILMS HAVE ALWAYS PROVIDED AN ESCAPE from the problems of real life. Even when it rained, and there was no money for the rent, the nearest cinema offered a fantasy world of love and romance where the sun always shone and birds sang. Screen romances matched the most unlikely couples, but the good guy *always* got the girl in the end. The course of love was never easy, and there was often heartbreak in the third reel, but usually tearful reunions in the last. Audiences called these films weepies, and classified them as one-, two-, or even three-hanky (handkerchief) films, according to how much they made people cry! Musicals, though, made everyone happy, and sent the audience home whistling the tunes. In a good musical there was a song or a dance round every corner. Even when disaster struck, the star glossed over the problems with a laugh, a catchy tune, and the patter of tap shoes.

LOVE NOSE NO BOUNDS
The French classic novel *Cyrano de Bergerac* was made into a film starring French actor Gérard Depardieu; it was a great hit. The tale of the ugly man with the huge nose, but the heart of a poet, seemed an unlikely success in the 1990s, although unrequited love and the death of the hero have always been a recipe for romantic success!

RAILWAY ROMANCE
Not every screen love affair has exotic locations and glamorous stars. The 1946 classic *Brief Encounter*, starring Trevor Howard and Celia Johnson, has an everyday backdrop (a station) that helps the audience identify with the characters, and imagine themselves in the same situation.

THE FACES OF LOVE
In 1979, the French Film Academy voted *Les Enfants du Paradis* (translated children of the gods, which is the name given to the cheap seats in the theatre) the best French film of all time. Certainly, it was one of the most romantic. Set in Paris theatreland in the 1840s, and made in German-occupied Paris in 1944, it explores the very different loves of four men for the same woman, and is as moving today as it ever was.

"AS TIME GOES BY"
In *Casablanca*, fine acting keeps the audience guessing who will get the girl, until the last scene. The director kept the superb cast guessing, too, and this suspense, and a memorable theme tune, helped make the film a romantic masterpiece.

THREE HANKIES
Many great romances were true three-hanky weepies, with tragic endings. In the 1936 film *Camille*, Camille, played by the famous romantic star Greta Garbo, dies in the arms of her lover – but she dies happy!

SNOW BUSINESS
Set in snowy Russia, *Dr Zhivago* is an epic love affair. Egyptian star Omar Sharif plays a Moscow doctor, and Julie Christie is the woman he loves and loses.

Fred Astaire is partnered by Cyd Charisse in *The Band Wagon*

FEVER PITCH
Musicals were most popular in the late 1940s and early '50s, but movies with music and dance still fill cinemas. Set in Brooklyn, the 1978 movie *Saturday Night Fever* starred John Travolta as a disco-dancing champ.

FRED AND GINGER
The greatest dancing team of the musical movie is undoubtedly Fred Astaire (1899–1987) and Ginger Rogers (born 1911). They first teamed up in the 1933 film *Flying Down to Rio*. Their dancing double act was so popular with the public that they made another nine films together over the next 17 years. Astaire was the better dancer, but his abilities were not recognized immediately: when he first auditioned, a studio talent scout wrote "Can't act, can't sing, slightly bald, can dance a little".

STAGE TO SCREEN
Many film musicals first appeared in a stage version, but few went on to be as successful as *The Sound of Music*, which broke box office records.

BASTILLE DAY
Like the shows they advertise, posters for musicals are bright, colourful, and full of fun. This poster promoted a 1933 musical by the French director René Clair (1898–1981).

UN · FILM · DE · RENÉ · CLAIR
14 JUILLET

DANCING FEET
Dance troupes, film companies, circuses, and performers of all sorts have masses of musical potential, so it is not surprising that they have formed the theme of many musical films. Many of the most charming sequences of the 1948 musical *The Red Shoes* are set backstage at a ballet.

Moira Shearer and Leonide Massine

KALEIDOSCOPE
American director Busby Berkeley (1895–1976) perfected the musical chorus in his 1930s films. In his films, dozens of dancers make whirling patterns of black and white for the camera.

Horses, heroes, and hoodlums

BIG JOHN
Even John Wayne (1907–1979) did not know how many Westerns he made. His career lasted over 50 years, and for most of that time he played a rugged cowboy who stood up for justice.

IN A WESTERN OR ADVENTURE MOVIE, even ordinary events seem exciting compared with life in a modern town or city. Saddling up a pony and riding off to herd cattle is a lot more thrilling than driving into town to buy dinner. And when the action *really* starts, screen adventures have more excitement in a minute than most people experience in a year. But through adventure movies we can experience all the drama we want from the comfort of a cinema seat. Action movies do not just provide excitement, though. Most are set in simpler times and places and make our own lives and choices seem trivial. So while we worry about what flavour pizza to order, the hero on screen faces real decisions, like the best way to fight off a hungry crocodile!

EASTERN WARRIORS
Japanese writer/director Akira Kurosawa (born 1910) produced in 1954 an exciting adventure film called *Seven Samurai*. The film became famous outside Japan only in 1960, when it was used as the basis for a much more famous Western *The Magnificent Seven*.

JOHN FORD
American director John Ford (1895–1973) made many milestone Westerns including 14 with John Wayne whom he made famous.

THE WILD WEST
Hollywood studios were fond of Westerns partly because the sets were free: the Wild West was literally just around the corner. Monument Valley in Utah was a popular location.

Water bottle is essential in desert conditions

Gun belt carried around 30 bullets

Repeating rifles could pick off enemies at 300 m (984 ft)

Most Westerns unfairly portrayed American Indians as at best, untrustworthy, or at worst, bloodthirsty savages. However, a few films, such as the 1950 movie *Broken Arrow*, and more recently *Dances with Wolves*, showed the Wild West from the Indian point of view

DESERT DARING

American frontier life provided Hollywood with perfect subject matter for exciting adventure movies. However, in other nations, the film industry did not have such a convenient home-made theme. For his 1962 film *Lawrence of Arabia*, British director David Lean (1908–1991) made an epic set in the deserts of the Middle East, and told the exciting story of T. E. Lawrence, a glamorous Englishman who led the desert peoples against their Turkish foe.

HERO FOR TODAY

American actor Harrison Ford (born 1942) has played daring hero Indiana Jones in three films. Though his adventures are never set in the Wild West, Ford's character shares many cowboy qualities: he performs noble deeds, and fearlessly challenges wrong-doers.

Raiders of the Lost Ark

SHOOT-OUT

The shoot-outs that are a familiar part of every Western are, in fact, fiction. Cowboy pistols were very inaccurate and deadly only at close range. They produced large clouds of smoke (not shown on screen) so after the first few shots the gunfighters would not have been able to see each other.

MOCK CROC SHOCK

Wise-cracking Australian Paul Hogan charmed cinema-goers all over the world as a crocodile hunter in *Crocodile Dundee*. The hero's adventures in the Northern Territory of Australia and in New York made the film the biggest box-office success ever to be made outside the USA.

Indian bows and arrows were inaccurate and had short range

Warren Beatty

Faye Dunaway

BONNIE AND CLYDE

The heroes of adventure films are not always the good guys. *Bonnie and Clyde* tells the story of a pair of bank robbers. They break the law and kill people, but they have the sympathy of the audience by the time they are gunned down in a police ambush.

THE DIRTY RAT

Like most of his roles, the character that actor James Cagney (1899–1986) played in *White Heat* is a violent gangster. The hoodlum dies as violently as he lived, in a spectacular explosion.

Into the unknown

BATMAN'S BAT Horror films have given bats, like this bat which appeared in the film *Batman*, a reputation as scary animals which they do not deserve.

Uɴᴋɴᴏᴡɴ ʜᴏʀʀᴏʀꜱ are much more frightening than those you see clearly. So in spine chillers and thrillers, every dark corner hides a menace or a monster. With luck it's a murderer or madman; without, it could be something much worse, like a vampire, or a steely skinned robot!

Horror movies began in Germany. As early as 1913, German film makers were frightening audiences with tales of artificial life and mysterious death. Hollywood took over in the 1930s, and in *Dracula* found a monster that has terrified movie-goers ever since. By the 1950s, rapid advances in science worried people more than any vampire. So film makers used people's fear of technology to create a new kind of film: science fiction. Today, horror and science fiction films appear in every imaginable form. But whatever the film, you can be sure that it's not mad axemen or alien androids that get the loudest screams – it's the *unexpected* peril lurking half-hidden in the shadows!

Christopher Lee, perhaps the most famous Count Dracula

PRINCE OF DARKNESS
In vampire movies, the soul of a dead man comes to life at night, and walks among the living, sucking their blood. The first vampire movie, *Drakula*, appeared in 1921. It was based on a book published 25 years earlier, and featured the exploits of Count Dracula.

Painted skin reveals veins and scales for extra reality

Latex rubber covers jointed limbs

Large jointed feet enable gremlin to be free-standing

Dracula's evening dress

SPACE SHAPES

Monsters from space have provided a theme for literally hundreds of movies, but one of the first and best was the 1953 film *It Came from Outer Space*. Originally made in 3-D for added drama, the film tells a now familiar story of aliens landing and adopting human shape.

STAB AND SLASH

Alfred Hitchcock's chilling 1960 film *Psycho* is a frightening murder story with a violent stabbing as the climax. The film is scary even when the story is known, and it was the first chiller to be shown as the main feature, not as the "B" movie (supporting feature).

ROBOCOP

Merging the cop movie with science fiction, *Robocop* plays on viewers' fear of both technology and inner-city crime. In the film an injured Detroit policeman is turned into a robot law enforcer.

GRISLY GREMLIN

Some of the most successful and scary horror films combine cosy familiar scenes with horrible frights. Just as the audience is beginning to relax, a monster pops up. *Gremlins* begins with a cosy Christmas scene in a town in the USA. An inventor gives his son a strange, but loveable furry creature called a mogwai. However, when certain care instructions are not followed, the furry creature produces some less pleasant offspring and these fierce gremlins reproduce rapidly and terrorize the town.

Drops of fake blood

FINGERS OF FEAR

In *Nightmare on Elm Street* children's bad dreams become reality, as they are chased by Freddy, a vicious monster with knife-blades for fingernails.

METALLIC MAIDEN

Open the props store at any film studio, and there's a good chance that a metallic android will fall out. German film maker Fritz Lang started the trend with robot Maria in his great 1926 movie *Metropolis*.

Klaus Kinski in *Nosferatu the Vampyre*, a 1979 Dracula re-make

STAR WARS

Elaborate special effects and a very fast-paced plot helped to make *Star Wars* the most successful science fiction movie in history. American director George Lucas made the film in 1977 mainly for people under 14 years of age, but the adventures of Luke Skywalker and his friends appealed to children and adults alike.

RE-VAMPED

The Dracula theme is one of the most popular in the history of movies. Only the detective Sherlock Holmes has appeared on screen more times than Dracula and his bloodthirsty family. The count has drunk human blood in more than 150 horror films, including *Billy the Kid meets Dracula* and *Love at First Bite*.

SPARE PARTS

In *Frankenstein* a scientist assembles a monster from pieces of corpses and uses a bolt of lightning to bring it to life. The fun starts when the creature escapes. Though more than 100 films have since used the theme, none has improved on the 1931 original which starred Boris Karloff as the monster.

Hope and glory

STANDING ON CEREMONY
The Oscar is reputedly so-called because it resembled a film librarian's Uncle Oscar. The ceremony began in 1929 as a celebration for guests from the film industry, but in 1930, it was broadcast on the radio (as seen above with Marie Dressler being congratulated by George Arliss and Norma Shearer), and today is a TV spectacular.

MOVIES ARE LIKE MODERN MAGIC SPELLS. They have enchanted the world from the first Kinetoscope flicker a century ago. Yet movie magic is unpredicatable and indefinable. Film companies spend millions making films with big-name stars, and millions more promoting them, only to see the film flop. Yet a cheaply-made film can rocket to success if it captures the public's imagination. For example, the 1979 Australian film *Mad Max* cost just $350,000 to make, yet earned its producers $100 million in just two years. Dreams of glory keep the hopes of film makers alive. And glory does not just mean money. Film makers compete for glittering prizes, such as Oscars (Academy Awards), which recognize that their film, or its cast and crew, is the best in the world.

BOMBAY BLOCKBUSTERS
Movies weave their magic spell most strongly in India. The Indian film industry, centred in Bombay, produces nearly 800 films a year – twice as many as the USA.

The Oscar is a gold-covered statue some 30 cm (13.5 in) high

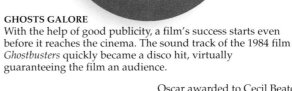

GHOSTS GALORE
With the help of good publicity, a film's success starts even before it reaches the cinema. The sound track of the 1984 film *Ghostbusters* quickly became a disco hit, virtually guaranteeing the film an audience.

VENETIAN VICTORY
Louis Malle's *Au Revoir les Enfants* won the top prize in 1987 at the prestigious Venice film festival. Also nominated for an Oscar, it was one of the most popular films of the year.

Oscar awarded to Cecil Beaton in 1964 for colour costume design for *My Fair Lady*

GLITTERING PRIZES
At numerous annual film festivals and ceremonies throughout the world, performers, directors, and technicians receive awards for being the best. These lavish ceremonies provide valuable free publicity for the films. The best-known awards are the Academy Awards, or Oscars given annually by the United States Academy of Motion Picture Arts and Sciences for the best film, best actor, best director, and many other categories. Oscar-winning films are more likely to succeed in the cinema, and even a nomination for an Award is an honour. Other important festivals are held in Berlin (Germany), and Cannes (France). But there are specialist film festivals, too, such as the Bhopal festival in India for children's films.

HOME RULE
Home Alone was the surprise hit of 1990. Its child star Macaulay Culkin was so popular that he was paid over two million pounds to star in the sequel, the most ever paid to a child star.

Chariots of Fire tells the story of two British athletes going for glory in the 1924 Olympic Games

"THE BRITISH ARE COMING"

The success of the 1981 British film *Chariots of Fire* was assured when it won prizes for best film, for best costumes, and for its music, by Vangelis. Best screen play Oscar went to its writer Colin Welland who brandished the award aloft with the words "The British are coming".

The *Palme d'or* (golden palm) is awarded for best film at the Cannes Film Festival

The best film at the Berlin Film Festival wins the Golden Bear

HYPE HELPS?

In movie industry slang, hyping a film means promoting it strongly. Clever hype is not always successful, but elaborate promotion and merchandising for *Batman* helped make it the studio's most successful film for 1989, the year it was released.

SPIN-OFFS

Films don't make money just from ticket sales. People who see the film often like to enjoy the plot again as a book and may also buy products based on the film, such as toys, T-shirts, and posters. The sale of these souvenirs, called merchandising, is very big business indeed.

ICONS AND IDOLS

Favourite movie stars seem to be perpetually young and beautiful: even when they grow old, they can always be seen at their best in old movies. Sometimes, dying young even helps the romantic image. James Dean and Marilyn Monroe were legends from the day they died and will still be screen idols 30 years from now.

Index

Acknowledgements

Dorling Kindersley would like to thank:

Leslie J. Hardcastle OBE, Janet Corbett and all the staff at the Museum of the Moving Image for their unfailing good humour and constant assistance. David Robinson for allowing us to photograph some of the objects displayed at MOMI, belonging to him. Rosemarie Swinfield for her make-up skills and the Charles Fox Make-up Studio for providing the make-up. Bermans International, Costumiers to the Entertainment Industry for providing many of the costumes. Farley for providing the props. Simon Crane and Sean McCabe for providing the stunt equipment and giving us the benefit of their

knowledge and experience. Joss Williams at Pinewood Studios and Martin Gutteridge, Graham Longhurst and all the staff at Effects Associates Ltd, Pinewood. Clare MacGillivray, consultant to Jim Henson Productions, and all the staff at Jim Henson's Creature Shop for bringing the creatures to life. Gerry Humphreys and Ursula Rains for their help at Twickenham Film Studios. All the staff at Hibbert/Ralph for the cartoons and for sharing their expertise. Céline Carez, Hannah Conduct and Helena Spiteri for editorial assistance. Liz Sephton and Cheryl Telfer for design assistance. Harriet Ashworth and Oliver Denton for research assistance.
Index by Jane Parker

Illustrations: Richard Ward/ Precision

Picture Credits
t=top, b=bottom, c=centre, l=left, r=right
Aardmans Animation/Channel 4 TV: 52bl, 53bl, 53br; Bayerisches National Museum 10tl; Bridgeman Art Library: 18tl, 24t; British Film Institute: 14tl, 15tl, 18tc, 19c, 19br, 20bl, 20cr, 21tl, 21cl, 21bl, 21tcr, 21bcl, 21bcr, 23c, 23b, 24tl, 27cr, 27cl, 28tc, 32bl, 33tc, 35tl, 35cl, 35cr, 35tr, 35c, 37t, 37bc, 37cr, 38bl, 39c, 39cr, 42tr, 42bl, 43tl, 43c, 44tl, 44bl, 46cl, 46cr, 50bl, 51br, 52cl, 52tr, 54bl, 55bc, 56cl, 56bl, 56cr, 57tl, 57cl, 57tc, 57c, 57tr, 57br, 58tl, 58tr, 59tl, 61cl, 61br, 61tl, 61br, 62bl, 63tl; Cliff Bolton for Twickenham film studios: 47tr; Zoe Dominic: 37bl; Mary Evans Picture Library: 6tl, 7tl, 7cl, 8br, 8cr, 10-11bl, 11cr; Joel Finler: 13tl, 15tr, 18bl, 19tc, 21c, 23c, 23cl, 23br, 25bc, 26tr, 27tc, 27br, 27cl, 33tl, 33c, 33br, 34tl, 38tl, 39tl, 39tr, 39b, 40tl, 43 br, 62tl; Ronald Grant Archive: 21tcl,

27bl, 28cr, 29br, 32cl, 33cl, 33bl, 43bl, 56cl, 59bl, 60cl, 61bl, 62cl, 62c; Henson Associates Inc. 1991: 44cr, 45bl: Hulton Picture Library: 11tl, 12tr; I.L.N. : 25br; KATZ/R. Lewis/Outline 29tc/Richard Foreman 40tr/Sven Arnstein 15cr/Sven Arnstein 42br; Kobal Collection: 10-11tl, 10cr, 12bc, 16tl, 16bc, 17bl, 19cr, 19bl, 20tr, 21br, 22br, 23tr, 23bl, 27bl, 27c, 28c, 30tr, 32-33, 34bl, 41br, 43tr, 49tl, 49cl, 50tr, 54tr, 55tc, 55br, 56tl, 56br, 57bl, 58tl, 59br; Kobal Collection/Lucasfilm Ltd: 35tc, 45tl, 45cl, 45tc, 48tlb, 59c, 61cr; M.P.L.12br; National Film Board of Canada: 52bl, 52c; National Museum of Photography, Film and Television: 13bl; National Portrait Gallery, London: 36tr; Oxbery: 45tr; The Post Office: 52cb, 52cr; Renaissance Films plc/photog. Sophie Baker: 47c; Anne Ronan Picture Library: 7bl, 11tcl, 12cl, 16cr, 23tc; Science Museum: 8cl, 9tl, 10cl, 10c, 12bl; J.D. Sharp: 24bc, 24bl, 24tl, 25t; Frank Spooner Pictures: 47cl; Zefa: 18cl, 18c, 58c.

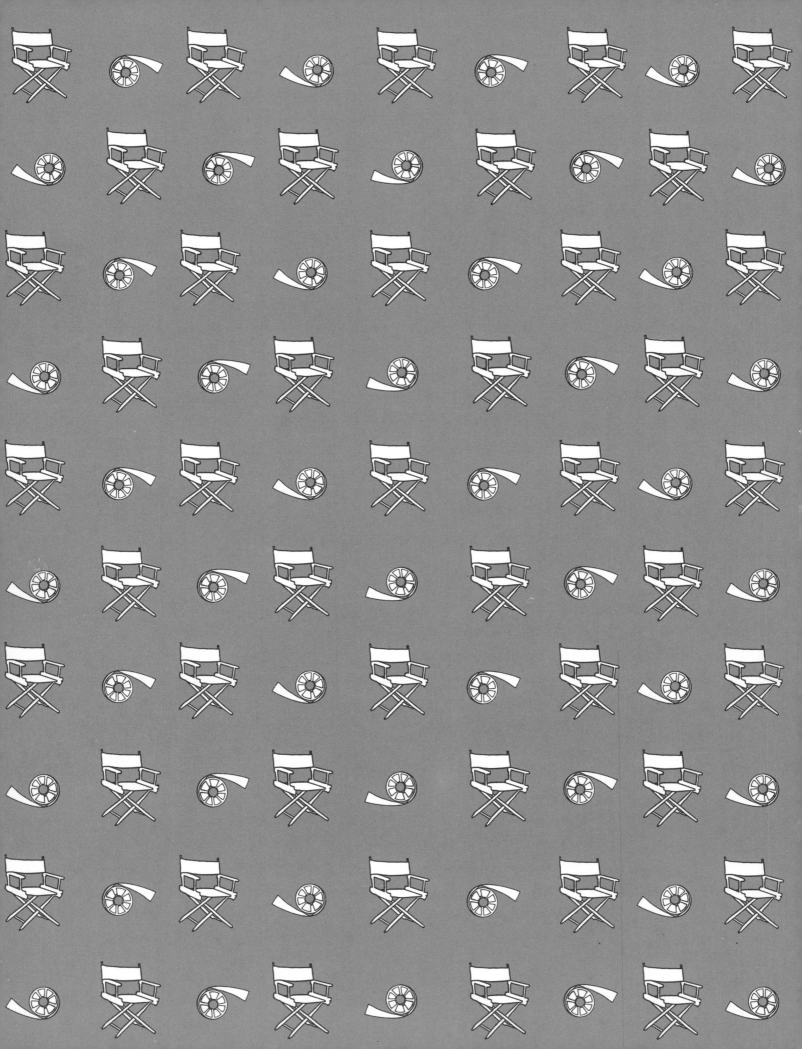